Japan in Southeast Asia: Collision Course

Raul S. Manglapus

 CARNEGIE ENDOWMENT FOR INTERNATIONAL PEACE
NEW YORK   WASHINGTON, D.C.

I.S.B.N. 0-87003-004-3

Library of Congress Catalog Card Number: 76-14709

Cover photo of January, 1974, anti-Japanese riots in Jakarta by World Wide Photos, Inc.; cover design by Shelia Freeman.

Printed in the United States of America

Table of Contents

PREFACE

The modern economic miracle has unquestionably been Japan, but in late 1973 and early 1974 two events — a double shock — cast doubt on the future stability of that nation's economic foundations. The first was the late-1973 oil embargo, which has been extensively examined elsewhere because of its effects on Japan and other oil-importing countries. The second shock occurred a few months later when Prime Minister Tanaka visited Southeast Asia on a good will mission.

Riots in Thailand and Indonesia greeted his arrival and stunned Japan. In Jakarta thousands of stores were damaged and a dozen people died. Mr. Tanaka was saved from personal injury only by extraordinary security measures involving a helicopter airlift from the palace where he was staying. Since then, the Japanese have begun to re-examine their policy toward Southeast Asia.

Precisely because Japanese policy toward that area has entered a period of transition, a study of Japanese-Southeast Asian relations seemed in order for the Carnegie Endowment's International Fact-finding Center, a program which supports investigative and anticipatory research, usually by journalists or diplomats, on near-horizon problems in international affairs. To undertake this study, the Endowment hoped to involve someone from Southeast Asia itself in order to reverse the usual pattern of the developed studying the developing.

The result is this study by Raul Manglapus, one of Southeast Asia's leading public figures. As a prominent Asian spokesman and writer, he has observed Japanese policy and practice in Southeast Asia both as an official and a student of international affairs. From 1954 to 1957, Mr. Manglapus served as Under-Secretary of Foreign Affairs of the Philippines, becoming Secretary in 1957. He was a senator from 1961 to 1967 and served as leader of the Progressives at the Constitutional Convention in 1971. Like many Filipinos, he was active in the World War II resistance movement against the Japanese. Standing on the battleship *Missouri* to observe the surrender ceremonies was one of the high moments of his life; yet he subsequently sent his son to Sophia University, where he graduated in 1971, an event which Mr. Manglapus recalls with great pride.

The value of his study is enhanced by this personal element. Mr. Manglapus benefits from a vantage point which would be difficult for an American or Japanese to adopt. Like others, he recognizes the tremendous contribution to this region which advanced nations, and particularly Japan, can make. At the same time, as a Southeast Asian, he may be more conscious of the politically explosive consequences which outside economic involvement at times may have.

Some of his recommendations are underlined by Chulalongkorn University professor Kien Theeravit in his study *The Japanese-Thai Economic Interaction*, a chapter of which Mr. Manglapus includes as an appendix to show that there is wide interest in the problems he discusses. As a Southeast Asian who wishes economic progress for its inhabitants, Mr. Manglapus seeks a new strategy of development which can insulate the region more effectively from the outside influences that he believes will inevitably undermine social and political stability and lay the foundation for future tension and confrontation with Japan.

Mr. Manglapus also sheds light on the sensitive and currently topical issue of commercial corruption. It was Gunnar Myrdal who contrasted in *The Challenge of World Poverty* the curious "disinterest among the great majority of economists" in exploring the effects of corruption in development with "the very lively interest [in this subject] shown in South Asian countries among the average literate people." He concluded that few issues penetrate the minds of people in developing countries like the issue of corruption.

Mr. Manglapus, by means of extensive interviews in the region, documents that this issue remains the most explosive and least understood aspect of developed-country relations with many countries in the developing world. Mr. Manglapus's study may therefore have relevance beyond Southeast Asia and Japan. His proposed development strategy is designed to increase the ability of all weak, developing states to combat through their own actions the negative effects of outside-inside corruption.

As always, Endowment sponsorship of the report implies a belief only in the importance of the subject. The views expressed are those of the author. Comments or inquiries on this and other work of the Endowment are welcome and may be addressed to the Carnegie Endowment for International Peace, 345 East 46th Street, New York City 10017 or 11 Dupont Circle N.W., Washington, D.C. 20036.

Thomas L. Hughes
President
Carnegie Endowment for
International Peace

I

Nanshin: Old and New

When the Japanese made their first significant appearance in Southeast Asia in the last hundred years, they were not perceived as aggressive invaders or predatory economic animals. They were viewed as liberators. When the first national Asian revolution against Western colonialism broke out in the Philippines in 1896, Japanese army reserve officers, artillery technicians, and ordnance and munitions experts were sent quietly to Manila to join the Filipino Revolutionary Army. They helped the Filipinos fight the Spaniards and later the American army which finally suppressed the first Philippine Republic.

Some of those Japanese were killed in battle. Others managed to return to Japan. In one colorful instance, a lieutenant from Tokyo, apparently an intelligence officer, fled a secret meeting, under raid by the Guardia Civil, through a subterranean exit behind the house of a Filipino *ilustrado* ("educated elite") in Intramuros, the walled city of Manila.

All this happened in the middle of the Meiji period (1867-1912), and it is not often mentioned, even in Japanese history books. It was an isolated case. The Filipinos were somewhat ahead of the times, and there were not too many movements of liberation in Asia to present Japan, just emerging from the Tokugawa seclusion (ca. 1603-1868), with occasions for probing actions in the region. The Japanese had not really made up their minds about Southeast Asia. They had as yet found no real use for what the area had to offer, though they were disturbed to see the aggressive moves of others.

Except for this first brief appearance in the Philippines, Japan's first "massive" *Nanshin* ("Southward Drive") was spearheaded largely by *karayuki-san*, i.e., prostitutes.

The Meiji government was quite content with this low profile in

Southeast Asia, but it had other plans in other directions. From the West, it wanted the Japanese to learn three things on which the new Japan might be built: constitutionalism, industrialization, and military organization. The large mission of government leaders to Europe and the United States led by Iwakura Tomomi in 1871 was followed by many more Japanese who were sent abroad to learn something useful.

In one generation, the societal balance and harmony that had flowered in the Tokugawa period prepared the nation to absorb all three institutions. Japan would still have to hurdle several coups and three wars before achieving a stable industrial economy. But at the turn of the century, it already had a constitutional government, an industrial complex, and a military machine. Having acquired all three, Japan was alerted to the possibilities—and the problems—of a stable industrialized power. Equality with Western nations now appeared a clear possibility. But industry must be fed with raw materials, and Japan, like England, has precious few of them. And a military machine must be given room to roll its armor, lest it rust away.

By the time Emperor Hirohito ascended the throne in 1926 and began the reign of *Showa* or bright peace, Japan had a new *Nanshin* under way. Southeast Asia, some Japanese economists can boast today, is not now and was not then Japan's only source of raw materials nor its only market. But geography is an irrefutable argument, and the Imperial Japanese Army was not in a position to conquer Brazil or Africa. China, the gateway to Southeast Asia, the love-hate cultural partner, ravaged by the Western powers and divided by indigenous war-lords, was just across the narrow sea, with enough land for military exercises, enough minerals for the mills, and enough people to provide an expanded market. There the Southward Drive began in full military fury.

Southeast Asia itself could wait to be inducted into the Greater East Co-Prosperity Sphere. It would first be conditioned with traders, bazaar keepers, gardeners. When the Imperial Japanese Army entered Manila in 1942, Japanese ice cream parlor operators quietly put on garments they had stored in wooden chests for years in anticipation of the day—officers' uniforms of the Imperial Japanese Navy.

I saw that *Nanshin* come to a humiliating end on the deck of the U.S.S. *Missouri* in September, 1945. Then I was a war correspondent attached to General Douglas MacArthur's headquarters. Today, the bitterness of the war is gone and my eldest son is a graduate of a Japanese university.

There were Filipinos in the underground during the war who swore that they had heard on San Francisco radio station KGEI, the Voice of America, a promise that after the victory the United States would strip Japan of its industrial plants and transfer them to the

Philippines. No one bothered to ask if this was logistically possible or whether the Philippines was prepared to operate these factories. There was only the naive hope that instant industrialization might indeed be a fitting reward for America's most hard-headed ally in Asia.

The Filipinos, along with the rest of the world, have since learned that in modern warfare the victors—certainly the victors' minor allies—do not necessarily inherit the spoils. It is not only that the victors seem to have become more humane, but also that there are other things to worry about, like balances of power, the heading-off of former major allies, ideological fears. Japan's postwar recovery and new *Nanshin*, more than the West German miracle, is the conclusive vindication of that ironic advice which was current in the fifties and which Peter Sellers attempted to immortalize in "The Mouse That Roared": For instant progress, declare war on the United States—and make sure that you lose.

Three days before Japan's formal surrender, a basic declaration of principles for its occupation was drafted by the U.S. Departments of State, War, and Navy. Remembering the lessons of Versailles, it conceded to the Japanese the "opportunity to develop an economy that would be adequate to meet their peacetime needs." There was to be no "transplanting" of industry to Southeast Asia. Though the *zaibatsu* ("family-controlled conglomerate") holding companies were to be dissolved, of 1,200 concerns marked for possible dissolution, only nine became the subject of the Supreme Commander's action. As we shall see, these nine would soon regroup in response to strong impulses in Japanese society.

The Japanese industrial network thus remained intact except that it was to be geared to "peacetime needs." A peacetime constitution was enacted which pledged that "land, sea and air forces, as well as other war potential, will never be maintained," thus relieving the state of the budgetary onus of national defense. The Japan-U.S. Security Treaty would provide Japan with free and adequate defense. The MacArthur land-reform program converted millions of share tenants into prosperous owner-cultivators and dramatically expanded the domestic market.

Under these hothouse peace conditions, Japanese industry began to take the only truly "great leap forward" in postwar Asia. Soon it was time to come to grips again with the problem that had propelled Japan into the war in the first place—the search for raw materials and an export market. And Japan again looked southward.

Professor Toru Yano, noted political scientist at Kyoto University asks, "How could Japan enjoy the freedom of action to advance into Southeast Asia after a war which was fought precisely in the same region had ended in Japan's defeat?" Japan had, Yano himself answers, a "windfall."

That windfall was the cold war. We had declared new enemies, and Japan was all the more rapidly absolved of its recent aggression. Japan was now an innocent bystander but with a difference. It was an active, not a passive, bystander, possessed of the capacity to profit from the preoccupations of its victorious enemies and their Southeast Asian friends, most of whom, along with the United States, were rather pleased to see it rise so wholesomely from defeat.

Because of the Korean and Vietnam wars, U.S. military procurements from Japan between 1951 and 1960 amounted to $6 billion. In 1966-67, at the height of the expanded Vietnam war, military contracts with Japanese firms came to over $500 million. That year, Japan's gross national product (GNP), which had risen the previous year by only 2.7 percent, jumped by 7.5 percent.[1]

The cold war had erupted into two hot ones, and both times Japan was at hand to sell the implements of hot war. Where the war remained cold and no overt invasions were in sight, the spectre of subversion by domestic insurgents loomed large and fearful. High on the list of preventive measures was the rush to provide the multiplying and expectant populations with "a better life." All this meant modernization, industrial and agricultural. And modernization meant a demand for capital and machines.

Both of these "implements of peace" the bustling Japanese economy could now supply. And as a defeated "aggressor," the only decent way Japan could begin supplying them was with a program of war reparations. Japan entered into reparations agreements with Burma, the Philippines, Indonesia, and South Vietnam. The total payments came to $1,152,800,000 in "damages," (i.e., machinery, equipment, and other goods), and $737,500,000 in loans. On the Japanese side, the program was actually conducted by the business community. The program served to recondition the people of the region to Japanese goods, Japanese spare parts, and Japanese practices—in brief, to a resurrected and refurbished Japanese presence.

This presence, scarcely twenty years after the graceful re-entrance, has become an omnipresence, and its continued growth appears irreversible. The omnipresence has bred resentment which may reach proportions capable of producing serious conflict in the area.

---

[1]Jon Halliday and Gavan McCormack, *Japanese Imperialism Today* (London: Pelican, 1973), p. 11.

II

Dimensions of the Presence

Trade

A country with territory about the size of the state of Montana, with no colonies and no natural wealth, is now the third largest industrial power on earth. With a GNP exceeding $400 billion, Japan ranks only after her victorious giant former enemies, the United States and the Soviet Union.

For a while, after the 1973 Organization of Petroleum Exporting Countries' (OPEC) embargo, the oil shock appeared to have shattered all optimistic predictions that had been made of Japan's future growth. Indeed, in fiscal year 1974-75, its real GNP growth slipped to −1.7 percent from a former five-year average of 12 percent. To the ordinary business-page prophet, this slip was acceptable evidence of Japan's extreme vulnerability to external economic forces. But it did manage a +6.1 percent growth in the midst of the energy crisis (1973-74), and by late 1975 it was clear that an apparently dismal minus performance in the fiscal year just ended had been in fact contrived; i.e., the government had tightened the money supply, limiting investments and imports with the avowed objective of controlling inflation. It was an overreaction, complained both Japanese domestic investors and foreign exporters, since Japan's 1974 rate of inflation of 18 percent, though it still made most Japanese unhappy, was then already among the lowest in the world. (By the end of 1975, it was down to a one-digit rate.)

The money squeeze was damned on both sides. Textile manufacturers complained that the market had been constricted and, when I was in Tokyo in January, 1975, were demanding import controls on cheap foreign textiles. At the same time, the Japanese press was gallantly publishing severe attacks on the policy from abroad, such as that by the articulate Briton, Derek Davies, editor of the *Far*

Eastern Economic Review. He thought the policy selfish and fatal to many medium-sized textile factories which the Japanese themselves had encouraged in Hong Kong, Taiwan, and other parts of Southeast Asia.

But the shoring-up operation was a success; the patient was alive and well and modestly admitting to a coming 5.6 percent growth in the current fiscal year (April 1976 to March 1977). "As an exercise in economic survival," said the London *Financial Times* in May, 1975, "Japan's achievement over the past year and a half deserves the envy not only of Britain but of practically every industrial nation whose economy was overwhelmed by the 1973 world oil crisis. It emerged . . . with an embarrassingly healthy trade balance, a moderate and decreasing rate of inflation and a promise of better things to come."

"Japan will grow much slower than before," Shijuro Ogata, the Bank of Japan's New York manager, said in a May, 1975, interview. "But," he added, almost as if he were ashamed to admit it, "she will grow a little bit faster than others."

This classic Japanese self-deprecation, so consistent that it sometimes is irritating, amuses the futurologists who now claim that their original predictions have been vindicated, namely, that Japan's dynamism would survive any kind of *shokku* ("shock"), whether from Nixon, the Arabs, or Lockheed, and carry her bounding into first position in the world economy before the turn of the century.

James Abegglen, whose Boston Consulting Group has reported to the British government that post-oil-shock Japan will grow at about 10 percent by 1980, said when interviewed in Tokyo: "A Westerner tends to discount whatever anyone says on the assumption that he might be boasting. So when a Japanese 'poor mouths,' the Westerner assumes that Japan must indeed be in a calamitous state."

Norman Macrae, deputy editor of the *Economist* (London), summarily dismisses the self-deprecative admissions and agrees with the 10 percent projection. He says in the January 14, 1975, *Economist*, "Growth has slowed shudderingly on five other occasions during [Japan's] twenty-five-year boom. Each time the wailing of the brakes and the warning about permanent slowdown have been quickly followed by reacceleration back to over 10% growth."

Robert Ballon, a Belgian Jesuit professor at Tokyo's Sophia University, is noted for his published analyses of Japanese business and is certainly another ardent member of the 10 percent-by-1980 club. He thinks that Japanese self-deprecation might mislead policymakers in other countries. He had a brief look at the draft of a study that was to form part of a coming report by an American research organization. The study stresses Japan's alleged extreme vulnerability, but Ballon thinks such a stress is "ridiculous and absolutely without scientific basis." The fact that the researcher commissioned to write the paper was Japanese may explain its pronounced pessimism.

The "little-bit-faster-than-others" growth that the Japanese admit so reluctantly for themselves will, according to the optimists, make Japan the largest industrial producer in the world by the 1990s. Macrae seems to be the most sanguine. By that time, he says, "the then 110 million Japanese would be more than twice as rich as the by then 220 million Americans."

Herman Kahn, noted futurologist in the Hudson Institute, is only slightly less sanguine. He had been expected to revise the optimistic predictions contained in his 1968 book, *The Emerging Japanese Superstate* (Englewood Cliffs, New Jersey: Prentice-Hall, 1970), down to more cautious proportions in view of the oil crisis. But in February, 1975, he announced he had been wrong in his prediction that Japan would overtake the United States in GNP by the year 2000. This will now happen, he said, in 1985. Unlike Macrae, he does not specify that the Japanese will be "more than twice as rich" as the Americans. He justifies his increased optimism by the remarkable adjustment of the Japanese to the oil crisis and world inflation. As Westerners, Abegglen, Kahn, and Macrae tend to assess Japan's progress mainly in the light of Japan's relations with the United States and Britain. They do not speak of the impact of this progress on Japan's relations with Southeast Asia—the focus of this study—which was a primary cause of World War II.

If these futurist projections are staggering, the present dimensions are impressive enough. Japan's high productivity has placed it in a commanding international position in the more important manufacturing activities, as illustrated in Table 1.

Japan is now the largest importer of raw materials in the world.

Table 1

Value of Japanese Output of Selected Products as a Percentage of Non-Communist World Output, 1965 and 1971

Products	1965	1971
Steel	13%	22%
Petrochemicals	12	18
Paper and pulp	8	11
Synthetic fiber	20	21
Automobiles	8	18
Electronics	6	14
Consumer electronics	13	38
Shipbuilding	46	50
Machinery	9	18

Source: Adapted from *Kogin Chosa* Report No. 1, 1974.

Barren of these materials, it is forced to import them to feed the voracious appetite of its giant industrial complex. The 1975 projections of Japan's import dependence for raw materials are detailed in Table 2. Japan has become the importer of 60 percent of all the raw

Table 2

Japan's Import Dependence for Raw Material

Raw Material	Estimated Import Dependence in 1975
Copper	82%
Lead	46
Zinc	57
Aluminum (Bauxite and Aluminum)	100
Nickel	100
Iron ore	91
Coking coal	92
Petroleum	92.9
Natural Gas	73.6
Uranium	100

Source: Centre for Strategic and International Studies, Jakarta.

products of the earth traded internationally. The other developed nations import 30 percent and the developing nations, 10 percent. Japan is also the largest single importer of oil. The Arab countries supply Japan 77 percent of its requirements; Indonesia supplies 14 percent. Japan imports 27 to 30 percent of the total Iranian output, 22 to 25 percent of the Kuwaiti, and about 12 percent of the Saudi Arabian. Indonesian sources report that 80 to 85 percent of their crude production goes to Japan. In 1970, Japan was already consuming 9 percent of the petroleum used in the noncommunist world, 14 percent of the copper, 11 percent of the aluminum, and 16 percent of the iron ores. The 1935 import of 26 million barrels of oil would have been used up in less than five days forty years later.

This almost total dependence on imported raw materials is ready grist for the "vulnerability" mill. Japan shares, in fact, a mutual vulnerability with its trading partners in the global market but enjoys a marked dominance over Southeast Asia and Australia.

Of the total of $62 billion in overall imports in 1974, $12.4 billion, or 20 percent, were from the Asian region. The five ASEAN (Association of Southeast Asian Nations) members (Indonesia, the Philippines, Singapore, Malaysia, and Thailand) accounted for $8 billion, or 12 percent. China accounted for $1.3 billion; Australia, $4 billion; and New Zealand, $400 million.

Japan has become the largest trading partner of all these countries with the exception of India and China. What, indeed, would

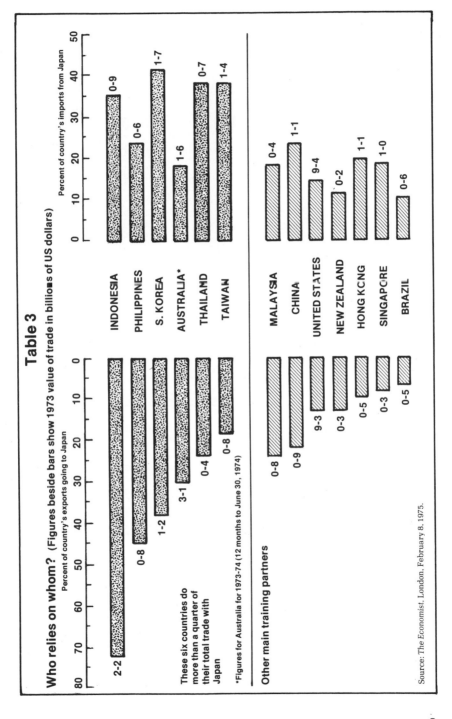

Table 3

Who relies on whom? (Figures beside bars show 1973 value of trade in billions of US dollars)

Percent of country's exports going to Japan

Percent of country's imports from Japan

Country	Exports	Imports
INDONESIA	2-2	0-9
PHILIPPINES	0-8	0-6
S. KOREA	1-2	1-7
AUSTRALIA*	3-1	1-6
THAILAND	0-4	0-7
TAIWAN	0-8	1-4

These six countries do more than a quarter of their total trade with Japan

*Figures for Australia for 1973-74 (12 months to June 30, 1974)

Other main trading partners

Country	Exports	Imports
MALAYSIA	0-8	0-4
CHINA	0-9	1-1
UNITED STATES	9-3	9-4
NEW ZEALAND	0-3	0-2
HONG KONG	0-5	1-1
SINGAPORE	0-3	1-0
BRAZIL	0-5	0-6

Source: The Economist, London, February 8, 1975.

9

Table 4

ASEAN Nations' Reliance on Trade with Japan (1972)

(In millions of US dollars)

Nations	Exports to Japan	Ratio to Total Exports	Imports from Japan	Ratio to Total Imports	Japan's Share in Total Exports and Imports
Indonesia	746	48.2	520	35.7	41.9
Malaysia	295	17.2	330	20.7	18.9
Philippines	373	33.8	391	31.8	32.8
Singapore	139	6.3	665	19.6	12.9
Thailand	233	20.7	570	36.9	28.8
Total trade of five nations with Japan	1,786		2,476		
Overall trade of five nations	7,676		12,130		
Japan's share in five nations' total trade	23.2%		20.4%		21.8%

Source: Centre for Strategic and International Studies, Jakarta.

Australia do with its iron and wool, Indonesia with its oil and logs, the Philippines with its copper and iron, Malaysia with its tin, or Thailand with its rubber if Japan stopped buying? They are Japan's satellites, says the *Economist* of February 8, 1975, and are unable to

Table 5

ASEAN Nations' Trade with Japan (1972)

Nations	Japan's Exports	*(In millions of US dollars)* Japan's Imports	Total
Indonesia	615	1,198	1,813
Malaysia	264	396	660
Philippines	457	470	927
Singapore	702	121	823
Thailand	522	252	774
Total of five nations (A)	2,560	2,437	4,997
Japan's total trade with Asia (B)	6,900	4,703	11,603
(A)/(B)x100 (%)	37.10%	51.81%	43.06%

Source: Centre for Strategic and International Studies, Jakarta.

Table 6

Japan's Trade with ASEAN Nations
(In millions of US dollars)

Exports

	1972	1973	Incr. %	1974	Incr. %
Indonesia	615.4	904.4	46	1,451	60.9
Malaysia	263.2	447.8	69	708.3	58
Philippines	457.4	620.2	35.6	911.5	47
Singapore	701.5	928.8	32.6	1,388	49.3
Thailand	522.1	719.9	37.9	951.9	32.2

Imports

	1972	1973	Incr. %	1974	Incr. %	Balance
Indonesia	1,197	2,213	84	4,568	106	−3116.6
Malaysia	395.5	776.2	96	979.3	26.2	−27
Philippines	470.3	820.2	74.4	1,103	34.5	−191.5
Singapore	120.9	223	84	618.9	177	+769
Thailand	252	393.6	56.2	685.3	74.1	+266

Sources: Compiled from information obtained from Nomura Research Institute.
MITI White Paper on International Trade, 1974, and Ministry of Finance.

---

dictate because "collectively they exert no more pull than individually . . . like Jupiter's moons."

"Who relies on whom?" asks the *Economist* and answers its own question in a table. The figures in that table, assembled from 1973 statistics provided by the Ministry of International Trade and Industry (MITI) of Japan and reprinted here as Table 3, show an astounding rate of dependence for the larger ASEAN nations like Indonesia (72 percent of exports, 35 percent of imports), the Philippines (45 percent of exports, 23 percent of imports), and Thailand (24 percent of exports, 37 percent of imports). The figures for 1972 from statistics of the ASEAN nations (Table 4) show a somewhat lesser but still impressive export dependence. The figures in Table 5 for the same year are from Japanese sources. They are substantially higher than those in Table 4, presumably because of differences in costs basis.

The more conservative figures from the five ASEAN nations in

Table 4 show a Japanese share of 21.8 percent in their total trade, 23.2 percent in their exports, and 20.4 percent in their imports. The Japanese statistics in Table 5 are even more revealing. They show Japan taking more than half of her Asian imports from the ASEAN countries. Viewed alongside Table 6 which contains figures for mid-oil-crisis 1973 and postcrisis 1974, one can capture some of the inexorable character of the exploding interdependence between Japan and the ASEAN nations.

The shoring-up operation inside Japan had included stepping up the export drive by manufacturing companies and cutting down on imports of light industrial products such as textiles. In May, 1974, Japan was suffering from a trade deficit of $1.3 billion. By June, 1974, this was down to $654 million. In December, 1974, Japan recorded a surplus of $581 million. This, of course, hurt its trading partners. But for oil, even Indonesia's trade advantage would have been erased.

Because of, among other things, superior credit facilities and greater market control, the industrialized partner in a trading relationship normally has the advantage over the supplier of raw materials. With the current notable exception of Arab oil, an agricultural or mineral supplier rarely enjoys a monopoly of supply, and the industrial buyer can go shopping elsewhere.[1] With this global hedge in Japan's hands, any leverage the Southeast Asians might have is further weakened and their dependence on Japan more total.

With the possible exceptions of Indonesia (to offset heavy oil imports) and Korea (for historical reasons), the evidence points to a deliberate global spread of Japanese export trade and investment. Global trade places Japan in a position to manipulate the trading process so as to allow itself flexibility in import sources. Australia now supplies half of Japan's iron ore. Australia enjoys the advantage of geographical proximity, but if the logistical obstacles were hurdled, Japan could turn to other trading partners to reduce its dependence on Australia: Brazil, which now supplies 11 percent of Japan's ore, India (15 percent), and South Africa (2 percent), assuming, of course, that the latter suppliers could develop surpluses to sell.

Even Japan's oil suppliers must be watchful. There are known untapped deposits in Latin America, the Sulu Sea, the Chinese mainland, and the East China Sea. There are also the ever-present prospects of sudden discoveries for the cheaper development of

---

[1] In April, 1970, I wrote in *Pacific Community*, a Japanese quarterly, that Southeast Asia could not take Japan for granted as a captive buyer of its raw materials since Japan had become, in fact, a global and not an Asian power. I quoted Gregory Clark, who said in *Asia Magazine*, "Japan is much more a global-minded than an Asian-minded power. For the Japanese, the primary concern is to keep open the avenues of international commerce to keep the world safe for Japanese trade."

other sources of energy. And Japan's options are magnified by its peculiar adroitness, in spite of obvious limitations of space and resources, in hopping in and out of crises and making quick changes with the tools of the free market economy to suit its immediate requirements. This adroitness is central to this study and will be the subject of later close scrutiny.

Investment

With these trade advantages in hand, the Japanese have entered the field of investment. Japan's overseas investments enjoy the same global hedge achieved for trade. The first postwar wave of investments penetrated North America and concentrated on the development of mineral sources. The United States remains the largest single recipient of Japanese investment, which now stands at $2.07 billion or 28 percent of the total of $7 billion in the global Japanese portfolio.

In the early seventies, Japan concentrated on Southeast Asia to exploit resources and cheap labor. Later, Brazil and Mexico began to offer Southeast Asia effective competition, and Brazil, perhaps by its sheer size and potential, has become the second largest host to Japan's investors.

Japanese approved overseas investment leaped from $844 million in 1971 to $2.5 billion in 1972, an increase of 200 percent. By mid-1973, the figure had jumped to $7 billion for another increase of 200 percent. (By contrast, U.S. overseas investment, which had stood at $84 billion in 1971, went up to $94 billion in 1972, an increment of 11 percent, and to $107 billion in 1973 for a 17 percent rise.) In relation to GNP, the rate of increase of Japanese overseas investment was equally significant. The $2.5 billion investment for 1972 was 0.7 percent of the year's GNP of $335 billion, while for 1973 the $7 billion investment was 1.6 percent of the $430 billion GNP, an increase of 0.9 percent. The United States remains the biggest single world investor, but the equivalent U.S. increase over the same period was only 0.2 percentage points, from 8.1 percent in 1972 ($94 billion investment, $1,155 billion GNP) to 8.3 percent in 1973 ($107 billion investment, $1,289 billion GNP).

The spectacular growth rate for Japanese foreign investment is even more startling in the light of a Nomura Research Institute report that Japan deliberately attempts to regulate overseas investment so that it constitutes about 25 percent of the value of Japanese exports, in line with its national policy of promoting exports. By contrast, Great Britain allows a ratio of over 100 percent of foreign investments over exports, and the United States, 200 percent.

MITI (Japan's Ministry of International Trade and Industry) has announced that approved Japanese overseas investments as of January, 1975, amounted to $10 billion, of which $4.5 billion had "materialized" by March, 1974. Of these $4.5 billion, 32 percent had

13

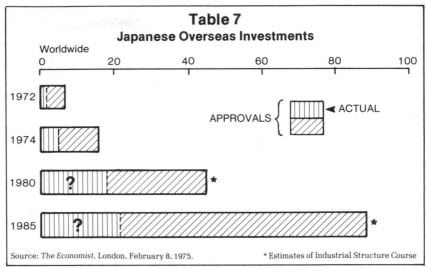

Table 7
Japanese Overseas Investments

Worldwide

Source: *The Economist*, London, February 8, 1975.   * Estimates of Industrial Structure Course

gone to ASEAN nations, distributed as follows: Indonesia, $.81 billion; Malaysia, $.2 billion; Singapore, $.17 billion; Thailand, $.16 billion; and the Philippines, $.13 billion. (A *Financial Times* dispatch in March, 1975, reported that the Philippine Board of Investments had announced that Japan had overtaken the United States as the largest annual foreign investor for the year 1974, putting in $79 million (34 percent) of that year's total inflow of $227 million, while the United States provided $41 million, only 18 percent of the total.)

MITI now predicts that Japan's direct investments will reach $45 billion by 1980 and $93 billion by 1985, in terms of today's prices. Table 7 shows the extent of this investment leap for the next ten years. In comparison with these projections, those of the futurologists seem quite conservative indeed. Abegglen, for example, suggests a cautious "range of probable projections" through 1980 of $28-$40 billion.[2]

The incarnation of the Japanese investment and trade presence is what is generally known as the *sogo sosha* or trading firm, which is perhaps the all-time understatement in the world of business. It is, in fact a mammoth empire of companies orbiting around a central core usually composed of a major bank, a commercial firm, an insurance company, and large industrial enterprises. If Douglas MacArthur were alive today, he would find it quite familiar but would probably wonder why it still exists, for he was supposed to have broken it up as Supreme Commander when it was still known as one of the *zaibatsu*.

MacArthur did "smash" the *zaibatsu*, but he had not counted

---

[2]Boston Consulting Group, *Japan in 1980* (London: Financial Times, Ltd., 1974), p. 141.

on certain impulses in Japanese society which would not be denied and which, displaying more effectiveness than all those king's horses and men who failed with Humpty Dumpty, put the giants back together again in fairly quick fashion. MacArthur's spirit may be consoled with a significant achievement, namely, that the concentrated family control over the giants is perhaps permanently gone. But the Japanese spirit, the group ethic, has proved quite unbreakable. The giants have quietly regrouped and slipped back into the world of commerce, and it has become a sort of pastime for foreign observers to find the best Japanese word to describe them. Some American business writers call them *keiretsu*, a term more properly applied to the leaders of business firms affiliated with the central core. Some Indonesian technocrats label them *zaikai*, which is strictly a term applicable to the leaders of the financial community. *Gyokai* is even less adequate since it properly describes leaders of specific industries. In the end, *guruppu*, the Japanization of "group," seems to be the best compromise.

These sprawling horizontal coalitions are not to be confused with the collaboration of a large manufacturing company with satellite suppliers of raw or semiraw materials and manufactured parts, a labor-distributive device quite common in industrial nations. Nor can they be identified as conglomerates in the American sense, since the members of the coalition are orbiters and collaborators and are not swallowed whole by a parent company.

Each member of the *guruppu* retains a modicum of real independence and, somewhat like autonomous states in a federal system, is able to contribute his own local initiative to the total energy. This autonomy exists in spite of considerable cross-ownership among members of the *guruppu*, not unlike the interlocking directorships and shareholders of U.S. corporations. For instance, among the major shareholders of Marubeni (capitalization, Y25 billion) are the Fuji Bank, the Sumitomo Bank, Yasuda Fire and Marine Insurance, and the Bank of Tokyo. Fuji Bank, in turn, is one of the major shareholders in Yasuda Insurance. (U.S. banks have shown a similar trend toward acquisition of large shareholdings in the more important corporations. IBM, for instance, with assets of $46 billion, lists seventeen U.S. banks among its stockholders with combined holdings in the billions of dollars, among them Morgan Guaranty, Bankers Trust, First National City Bank, Chase Manhattan, Chemical Bank, and the Bank of America.)

The competitive advantage of these bank-centered groups in such large-scale activities as petrochemicals is summarized by Harvard Business School Professor Michael J. Yoshino as follows:

> *First*, the cooperative approach enables the participating firms to share the risks associated with a large-scale project. *Second*, the group's banks are quite willing to support joint

projects sponsored by several firms within their group, so the venture has ready access to financial resources and is thereby able to overcome a critical entry barrier in petrochemicals—the large capital requirement. *Third,* such an arrangement can be an important asset in negotiating with the host government, since it puts the Japanese in a position to offer an integrated package,[3] from ethylene production to downstream operations. *Fourth,* the presence of a trading company at the core gives the Japanese petrochemical ventures several distinct advantages. The trading company brings critical skills for negotiating and organizing large-scale ventures abroad not possessed by petrochemical manufacturers. Also, the multinational network for the trading company helps to provide the ventures with export opportunities, thereby enabling them to enjoy further economies of scale. Basic petroleum products are well suited to distribution through trading companies. *Finally,* the trading company can assist in developing the market for petrochemical products locally by assisting its Keiretsu downstream processors and fabricators to establish plants within the country.[4] [Italics added]

With these advantages in hand, the groups have become the leading traders, producers, and investors in Japan.

A central management council, the *kai,* plans each group's total strategy. These are properly the *keiretsu,* the top men in the core companies of the group. They direct the policies of companies of various activities and sizes. In the Furukawa group there are thirty-two member companies. There is a Mitsui *Shoji* ("trading company"), a Mitsui Bank, a Mitsui Mining and Smelting Company. Between them, the groups dominate the foreign trade and the domestic and foreign investments of Japan.

The heavy investment presence in the ASEAN countries in the context of a convenient global spread is illustrated in the listing in Table 8 of the twenty top-ranking overseas manufacturers. With the exception of three firms, every one has invested in at least two of the five ASEAN countries.

Japanese global overseas investment is not limited to manufacturing activities such as electronics, wood processing, and precision equipment, which the Japanese have dominated for the past two decades. They now range far into other activities such as real estate, warehousing, banking, transportation, and communication.

---

[3] Not to be confused with the "package deal" embracing financing, know-how, supplies and policy decisions.

[4] Michael Yoshino, from a manuscript soon to be published and tentatively entitled "The Multinational Spread of Japanese Enterprises: Strategy and Structure" (Cambridge: Harvard University Press, late 1976 or early 1977).

16

Table 8

Ranking Japanese Overseas Manufacturers

	1973 Overseas Production ($100M)	Foreign Subsidiaries	Major Countries	Major Products
1. HITACHI	179	20	Taiwan, Hongkong, Philippines, Thailand, Malaysia, Singapore, Argentina, Chile, West Germany	Appliances
2. MATSUSHITA	179	45	Korea, Taiwan, Phillippines, Thailand, Malaysia, Singapore, Indonesia, West Germany	Electronics
3. YOSHIDA	120	27	Taiwan, Hongkong, Thailand, Malaysia, Indonesia, France, Holland, Canada, USA	Zippers
4. JANYO	118	28	Korea, Taiwan, Hongkong, Philippines, Thailand, Malaysia, Singapore, Indonesia, Spain	Electronics
5. TEIJIN	116	25	Korea, Taiwan, Hongkong, Philippines, Thailand, Singapore, Indonesia, USA, Brazil	Fabrics
6. TOYOTA	93	10	Thailand, Indonesia, Singapore, USA, Canada, Brazil, Costa Rica, Peru	Cars
7. NISSAN		12	Thailand, Malaysia, Singapore, Turkey, Canada, USA, Mexico, Peru	Cars
8. MITSUBISHI HEAVY INDUSTRY	81	18	Taiwan, Thailand, South Vietnam, Singapore	Ships
9. AJINOMOTO	75	11	Philippines, Thailand, Malaysia, Indonesia	Food
10. TOYO MILLS	70	25	Singapore, Indonesia, USA	Textiles
11. ISHIKAWA	69	8	Malaysia, South Vietnam, Singapore, Brazil, Peru, Australia	Ships
12. UNITICA	61	18	Taiwan, Hongkong, Thailand, Malaysia, Singapore, Indonesia, Brazil	Fabrics
13. TORAY	52	46	Korea, Taiwan, Hongkong, Thailand, Malaysia, Singapore, Indonesia, UK	Fabrics
14. TOSHIBA	51	22	Korea, Taiwan, Hongkong, Philippines, Thailand, Malaysia, India, Iran, Canada, USA	Electronics
15. DAI NIPPON	45	11	Hongkong, Malaysia, Singapore, Brazil	Printing
16. MITSUBISHI ELECTRIC	41	26	Korea, Taiwan, Hongkong, Philippines, Thailand	Electronics
17. KANEBO	36	16	Korea, Taiwan, Hongkong, Thailand, Indonesia	Textiles
18. HATTORI	36	10	Taiwan, Hongkong, West Germany, UK, Canada	Seiko watches
19. NIPPON ELECTRIC	33	18	Korea, Taiwan, Iran, USA, Brazil	Communications
20. TEAC	31	4	Hongkong, USA	Audio

Source: Nomura Research Institute, New York.

17

Table 9
Japanese Overseas Investment by Industry

| | 1973 | | | | | | 1974 | | | | | |
	A Already operating	B Planning	C Not Planning	D Unknown	E TOTAL	A+B / E	A Already operating	B Planning	C Not Planning	D Unknown	E TOTAL	A+B / E
Total Industries	470	97	629	464	1660	34.2	530	112	686	367	1695	37.9
Agriculture & fisheries	7	0	0	0	7	100.0	7	0	0	0	7	100.0
Mining	5	2	7	0	14	50.0	5	2	6	0	13	53.8
Construction	17	7	56	34	114	21.1	23	12	59	30	124	28.2
Manufacturing	328	70	409	292	1099	36.2	372	81	440	216	1109	40.8
Food	19	4	35	29	87	26.4	23	6	39	20	88	33.0
Fabric	34	3	20	30	87	42.5	44	4	31	9	88	54.5
Pulp	10	3	12	10	35	37.1	11	5	14	5	35	45.7
Chemistry	55	9	52	52	168	38.1	57	15	51	45	168	42.9
Oil, coal	3	1	6	2	12	33.3	3	0	6	3	12	25.0
Gum	6	1	7	6	20	35.0	7	1	8	4	20	40.0
Glass & china	11	4	28	22	65	23.1	13	2	31	19	65	23.1
Steel	15	3	28	21	67	26.9	16	2	30	19	67	26.9
Non-metal	16	2	17	5	40	45.0	16	4	16	4	40	50.0
Metal	4	4	34	12	54	14.8	5	3	35	12	55	14.5
Machine	38	12	71	44	165	30.3	47	13	76	29	165	36.4
Electrical equipment	64	13	45	28	150	51.3	73	14	47	20	154	56.5
Transport equipment	25	5	31	14	75	40.0	25	9	31	12	77	44.2
Precision equipment	14	4	9	6	33	54.5	16	2	10	5	33	54.5
Others, manufactures	14	2	14	11	41	39.0	16	1	15	10	42	40.5
Commercial	53	9	34	32	128	48.4	56	9	35	35	135	48.1
Banking	25	2	42	42	111	24.3	28	3	61	28	120	25.8
Real estate	6	1	4	7	18	38.9	6	0	6	7	19	31.2
Transportation	19	2	28	27	76	27.6	22	3	30	21	76	32.9
Warehouse	6	1	16	6	29	24.1	6	2	15	6	29	27.6
Communication	0	0	3	3	6	0	0	0	3	3	6	0
Electrical, gas	0	0	16	2	18	0	0	0	11	7	18	0
Service	4	3	18	15	40	17.5	5	3	20	11	39	20.5

Source: Nomura Research Institute, New York.

Table 10

Japanese Foreign Investment

| | Accumulated Stock of Direct Foreign Investment | | | | | | | | Total Accumulated Stock of Foreign Investment | | Total Amount of Overseas Production | | Employees of Japanese Enterprises 1985 | |
| | 1973 | | 1980 | | 1973-80 | 1985 | | 1980-85 | 1980 | 1985 | 1980 | 1985 | Total | Japanese |
	US$ millions	Percentage Distribution	US$ millions	Percentage Distribution	Average Growth Rate %	US$ millions	Percentage Distribution	Average Growth Rate %	US$ millions	US$ millions	US$ millions	US$ millions	People 000	People 000
Agriculture, forestry and fisheries	229	2.2	600	1.3	14.8	1,560	1.7	≤1.1	1,200	3,120	250	660	65.8	4.5
Mining	3,061	29.8	14,380	32.0	24.7	30,340	32.4	-5.1	28,760	60,680	7,470	15,770	163.1	8.6
Timber and pulp	362	3.5	2,740	6.1	33.4	5,510	5.9	-5.0	5,480	11,020	4,000	8,040	96.4	2.0
Sub-total	3,652	35.6	17,720	39.5	25.3	37,410	40.0	-6.1	35,440	74,820	11,720	24,470	325.3	15.1
Foodstuffs	167	1.6	400	0.9	13.3	960	1.0	-9.4	800	1,920	1,010	2,440	31.7	0.5
Textiles	743	7.2	1,440	3.2	9.9	2,700	2.9	13.4	2,880	5,400	2,590	4,860	240.7	3.8
Chemicals	538	5.2	4,070	9.1	33.3	8,600	9.2	-6.1	8,140	17,200	5,370	11,350	92.0	3.1
Iron and steel and non-ferrous metals	486	4.7	4,650	10.4	37.9	12,840	13.7	22.5	15,500	42,800	19,530	53,930	288.3	2.9
General machinery	217	2.1	600	1.3	15.6	980	1.1	-0.2	1,200	1,960	2,770	4,530	57.6	1.3
Electric machinery and appliances	328	3.2	1,560	3.5	25.0	2,920	3.1	-3.4	3,120	5,840	6,240	11,680	153.8	1.8
Transport machinery	222	2.2	630	1.4	16.1	1,020	1.1	-0.1	1,260	2,040	1,260	2,040	25.7	0.5
Other manufacturers	197	1.9	2,210	4.9	41.2	3,940	4.2	-2.3	4,420	7,880	5,650	10,080	178.5	3.9
Sub-total	2,898	28.2	15,560	34.7	27.1	33,930	36.3	-6.9	37,320	85,040	44,420	100,910	1,068.3	17.8
Construction	67	0.7	140	0.3	11.1	230	0.3	-4.9	280	560	780	1,570	32.5	1.3
Commerce	1,232	12.0	3,560	7.9	16.4	7,290	7.8	-5.4	3,960	8,100	3,760	7,690	458.5	45.9
Finance and Insurance	917	8.9	2,840	6.3	17.5	5,790	6.2	-5.3	3,160	6,430	1,800	3,660	83.9	16.9
Miscellaneous	1,504	14.6	5,050	11.3	18.9	8,810	9.4	-1.8	10,100	17,620	16,260	28,360	972.5	22.4
Sub-total	3,720	36.2	11,590	25.8	17.6	22,170	23.7	-3.8	17,500	32,710	22,600	41,280	1,547.4	86.5
TOTAL	10,270	100.0	44,870	100.0	23.4	93,540	100.0	5.8	90,260	192,570	78,740	166,660	2,941.0	119.4

Source: Far Eastern Economic Review, November 29, 1974.

The Japanese banks enjoyed a share of almost 21 percent of the medium- and long-term market by May, 1974. Table 9 shows the range of operating activities and the number of operating plants abroad in each category. The MITI projection (see Table 10) of $45

Table 11

Top Overseas Ventures

Country	Company	Ratio of Japanese Investment	Industry
Canada	Toyota Motor (Sales Industry) /Mitsui Product	87.26	Import of motor cars, assembly and sales
Australia	Nissan Motor Co.	100	KD* production of motor cars
Greece	Nippon Kokan K.K./C. Itoh Co.	60	Steel
USA	Alaska Pulp	100	Logging
Mexico	Nissan Motor/Marubeni	100	KD production of motor cars
Thailand	Toyota Motor (Sales Industry)	82	Import of motor cars, assembly and sales
Taiwan	Sanyo Electric Co.	49	Electric appliances
Taiwan	Hitachi	100	TV, tape recorders
Australia	Toyota Motor (Sales Industry)	50	Import of motor cars, assembly and sales
Canada	Honshu Paper, Inc./Mitsubishi Co.	50.04	Wood pulp, logging
USA	Mitsubishi Heavy Industries /Mitsubishi Co.	100	Production, sales of airplane parts
Korea	Teijin Co.	50	FY* production
USA	Alaska Pulp	100	Pulp
Taiwan	Matsushita Electric Co.	60	Electric appliances
Hong Kong	Daidov Maruta Senkou Co. /C. Itoh Co.	45	Dyeing adjustment
Taiwan	Teijin Co.	40	FY production (polyester)
Brazil	Ihi Co.	96.6	Ships, heavy machinery
Thailand	Isuzu Motor/Mitsubishi Co.	85	KD production of dump body
Korea	Toray Industries	45	Nylon cloth
Korea	Toray Industries/Mitsui Products	50	Rayon cloth
Brazil	Sumitomo Metal Co./Sumitomo Shuji	40	Motor car parts
New Zealand	Showa Electric Industries/Sumitomo Chemical Industries	50	Aluminum

billion in foreign investment by 1980 and $93 billion by 1985 shows investments spread among various industry categories all of which will experience average growth rates.

The investment share of the Japanese in overseas ventures ranges from 40 percent to 100 percent. However, effective control is retained even in cases of less than 50 percent participation by the operation of local corporation laws or by control of credit, tech-

Korea	Toray Industries/Mitsui Products	50	Polyester
Korea	Hitachi Electric Wire Industries	47	Electric wire cable
West Germany	Janome Sewing Machine Industries	50	Production, sales of sewing machines
USA	Yoshida K.K.	100	Zippers
Peru	Nissan Motor/Marubeni	75.5	KD production of motor cars
Brazil	Teijin/Marubeni Co.	50	Polyester
Brazil	Kanebo	72.3	Production, sales of cotton yarn
Malaysia	Toyo Industries/Sumitomo Co.	41.4	KD production of motor cars
Korea	Sanyo Electric Co./Sumitomo Co.	50	TV, radio
Australia	Sanyo Electric Co.	50	TV, stereo
Thailand	Toray Co./Mitsui Products	50	Nylon
Puerto Rico	Matsushita Electric Co.	70	Electric appliances
Brazil	Tochiku Spinning Co.	100	Cotton spinning
Taiwan	Funai Electric Co.	100	Transistor radios
Thailand	Shikishima Spinning Co./Nomura Trade Co.	50	Cotton spinning, production of blankets
Philippines	Teijin Co./Tomen	40	FY, SF* production of polyester
Thailand	Teijin	50	FY, SF production of polyester
Mexico	Nippon Steel/Mitsubishi Co./Mitsui Products	15	Iron manufacture
Canada	Jujoyo Paper Industries/Sumitomo Forestry Co.	75	Lumbering, production of pulp
Brazil	Furukawa Electric Industries/Mitsui Products	100	Electric wire cable
Thailand	Mitsui Products/C. Itoh Co.	40	Production, sales of GI* sheets
Thailand	Toray Industries/Tomen/Gisen	48.4	Polyester
Thailand	Teijin/Fuji Spinning Co./Toyota Trade Co.	45.45	Spinning
USA	Sumitomo Metal Industries	60	Steel pulp
Brazil	Tomen	100	Refining of peanuts
Colombia	Kawasaki Steel/Mitsubishi Co.	49	Electric tin plate
Canada	Kobe Steel Manufacture Co./Mitsui Products/Jinko Wire Industries	79.3	Steel
Singapore	Eidai Industries Co.	55.5	Board

Source: Nomura Research Institute, New York

*KD (Knock-down); FY (filament yarn); SF (synthetic fiber); GI (roofing).

nology, etc. The listing of top overseas ventures in Table 11 demonstrates the range of Japanese participation in capitalization; of the fifty listed, eleven are 100 percent Japanese owned.

The economic dimensions of Japan's world stature can perhaps be best summed up in its dealings with the World Bank. From 1953 to 1966, Japan was the biggest borrower among the member nations of that United Nations agency, obtaining a total of thirty-one loans worth $863 million, mostly for infrastructure and heavy industry. In 1966, Japan began to lend to the Bank for its capital. By 1974, it had become the biggest annual lender to the Bank with total lendings for that year of $1.8 billion. Table 12 demonstrates the overwhelming

Table 12

World Bank Borrowings by Country in Fiscal 1974

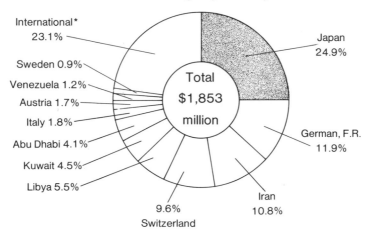

*Two-Year Bond issues placed with central banks, governmental agencies and with international organizations.

Source: Ministry of Foreign Affairs, Tokyo, December, 1974.

Japanese presence in the Bank's borrowing portfolio for 1974. While these figures are not cumulative and represent only the borrowings in fiscal year 1974 (World Bank sources indicate insignificant borrowings from the United States in that year), they do illustrate Japan's dramatic graduation from borrower to lender. To update Frank Gibney's cryptic picture of the new economic giant,[5] Japan is now factory, trader and lender to the world. It certainly is all of that to Southeast Asia; the peoples of the region have only begun seriously to ask how it happened so quickly—only two decades after the devastation of war.

---

[5]Frank Gibney, Japan, the Fragile Superpower (New York: W. W. Norton, 1975). p. 19.

The awesome and, for some Southeast Asians, disquieting dimensions of the Japanese presence have been picturesquely described by Yoshio Murakami, *Asahi* correspondent in Bangkok, whom I interviewed in January, 1975, as those of "a huge battleship coming into a little pond." Explaining why some conflict is inevitable in spite of due care by the Japanese, Murakami said, "The battleship thinks that it is moving very slowly and carefully in order not to cause any trouble; but its slightest move creates waves which topple a lot of little ships around."

How the battleship got to be so huge is the first challenging question. In the search for answers, fact and fancy, truth and speculation, have not been unmixed. It is perhaps time to do some weeding. For there is really nothing very special about the Japanese people. There appears, however, to be something very special about Japanese social organization.

III

How the System Works

Japanese Global Enterprise

The *Défi Americain* preoccupied Europeans in the sixties. Its expanded version—the Multinational Threat—is bothering an increasing number, including Americans, in the seventies. Some, like Richard Barnet, director of the Institute for Policy Studies and co-author with Ronald Müller of *Global Reach,* would unmask the U.S. multinational as not a multinational at all, unlike some of its European cousins, but an American-owned enterprise with a global strategy and a planetary appetite which transcends, and indeed is in the process of destroying, not only national planning but the nation state itself, a prospect that pleases some and alarms others.

The defenders of the U.S. global enterprise regard it as the new and only possible, realistic, and productive internationalism that is bound to supplant the obsolete political structures of the world in its irreversible drive to maximize the use of the earth's materials for the benefit of all mankind. It has, on the other hand, been charged with attempting to bring down or, in cooperation with government agencies, successfully bringing down foreign governments. It also stands charged with abetting corrupt dictatorships and underwriting repression, with its artificial stimulation of appetites for unnecessary consumer goods, enrichment of the elite and impoverishment of the masses, and creation of false fronts of prosperity without real development.

The Japanese global enterprise is under indictment on all of these counts except perhaps that of attempting to bring down governments (although, as we shall see, its activities can provide the setting, occasion, or stimulation for movements that have attempted to bring down or have actually brought down governments). It is suspected of almost all the refinements of the questionable practices of global enterprises, including, as will be detailed later, the use of the banked savings of the local population for its operations and the

24

extraction and withdrawal of these savings from the country as profits, with the resulting depletion of foreign exchange reserves.

It could be useful to analyze these suspicions, for we stand on the edge of an era when, as Japan's economic power grows, Japanese enterprises seem certain to expand and cover the earth as rapidly as has the U.S. global enterprise in the last two decades. Some lessons might emerge from the analysis and examination to help in avoiding the mistakes of the past two decades, whatever one's views might be of these enterprises.

Yet the Japanese challenge is not easily decipherable. It is unique and, therefore, perhaps more fearful to vulnerable societies because the Japanese global enterprise, unlike its American counterpart, is not really one individual, though giant, enterprise competing with its fellow individual national or foreign enterprises. The Japanese challenge is not the Japanese corporation. It is not a group of competing corporations. It is not even "Japan, Incorporated," if that is taken to mean only the total cooperation between corporations, the flawless collaboration between the giant groups. The Japanese challenge is Japan itself, a solid, homogeneous, harmonious, cooperative unit engaged in world business. History, tradition, culture, idiosyncracy have combined to weld all the active branches of Japanese society—the universities, the banks, the trading companies, the manufacturers, the government, the trade unions, the family—into one business operation.

When, for instance, an Indonesian businessman thinks he has an interesting proposal for food processing, he may approach Ajinomoto. Ajinomoto will then refer the proposal to the Mitsubishi Trading Company which is at the top of the group to which Ajinomoto belongs. The Mitsubishi branch or liaison office will undertake the planning, development, and negotiation of the venture. Before the arrangements become final, the Indonesian may find that he has been dealing not only with Ajinomoto and Mitsubishi but also with Mitsui and Marubeni whom Mitsubishi has invited into the enterprise in order to broaden its support and insure its stability.

Indonesian businessmen are normally short of capital. It is not easy for them to borrow from Indonesian private or government banks. Interest rates are prohibitive, particularly for local entrepreneurs with limited personal resources or collateral. The Mitsui Bank saves the day with a medium-term loan, both for capitalization and operating expenses. The loan does not go directly to the Indonesian partner but is channeled through the intermediary firms which have provided the guarantee. The Mitsui Bank, in turn, need not worry about overloaning as much as other foreign banks. The Bank of Japan (Central Bank) is always ready to back it up. The interest on the loan is at the level of or lower than normal international rates. But the low interest rate may have been compensated for in the higher amount paid for equipment and machinery which will come from Japan and perhaps in the higher price of raw materials which are probably grown and/or distributed by a sister Japanese firm.

A few more items complete the package deal. Technology for the processing will come from Japan, applied by Japanese technicians, providing the Japanese partner with even more effective managerial control. Finally, the finished product may have to be offered for priority purchase or distribution by sister firms in Japan. Approval for the package comes from the Ministry of International Trade and Industry which has the general power of allocation of resources for foreign investment.

In the end, the Indonesian finds that his partner in the venture is not just another Japanese, not just another Japanese firm, not just a consortium of food processors, insurers, banks, traders, not even Japan, Incorporated. His partner is Japan.

Alone and overwhelmed, he finds himself unable to exercise a respectable modicum of influence in the management of the company. Even if he had initially chosen to attempt to extract the best bargain by playing one Japanese firm against another, by trying to "divide and conquer," he would have failed, for one cannot play one Japanese firm against another.

One does not land a job with Sumitomo by presenting a plan on how to destroy Mitsubishi. It is not Sumitomo's consuming ambition to get rid of Mitsubishi. Sumitomo prefers to reach an understanding, a consensus, with Mitsubishi and all the other groups, particularly on overseas business. That this is, in fact, better for business is not the underlying reason for this urge to consensus. That it is better for Japan is closer to the truth but not the whole story. When the big companies move toward consensus, they are simply being Japanese. The interdependence, the strength through unity, the quality of indivisibility which leads to unconquerability in business, all are the by-products of being Japanese, or better, of being members of Japanese society.

The Vertical Ie

The subservience of individualism to the community has been traced by some to the history of wet rice cultivation. In Japanese villages, the theory goes, rice cultivation was always a cooperative process. So it seemed natural that this should lead ultimately to the modern "tribalism," the work ethic, and interdependence. Unfortunately, this theory does not explain why the same results did not come from wet rice cultivation in the Philippines, for example, where it has also been a traditional process but where the *bayanihan*, the village community spirit, is not reflected in the national ethos.

Japanese homogeneity is the product of a unique combination of geographic and historical forces. Protected by inhospitable seas, the archipelago was spared the massive cultural infiltration that was the common lot of smaller nations on the Asian mainland. During the Jomon period (from the fourth or fifth millenium to ca. 250 B.C.), a uniform culture spread throughout the country. Considerable mainland influence, mostly Chinese, then crossed the seas, including wet paddy cultivation. Some migration occurred which was minimal and quickly absorbed into the indigenous population. From the beginning of the historical era (fifth century), evidence of alien entry into the population began to disappear.

From that time on, the native culture flourished, permitting only slight variations and nuances in language and tradition. In 1603, the *daimyo* ("feudal lord") Tokugawa Ieyasu, having defeated his fellow *daimyos* in battle, succeeded in establishing a centralized military government *(shogunate)* with headquarters, or *bafuku*, in Edo, the ancient Tokyo. What was already a basic cultural homogeneity was institutionalized under a central feudal system with an emperor as the symbolic apex but not the effective ruler of the unified nation. Japan was unified under the rule of the *shogunate*.

At the base of the nation were the peasants who comprised 00 percent of the population. The *samurai*, comprising 6 percent, were salaried hereditary bureaucrats and contributed, as the administrators and intellectuals of the system, to the broad formation of a uniform tradition. The rest of the population consisted of merchants, priests, craftsmen, and insignificant minor groups.

There were no widely separated classes of poor and rich, no gentry. The *samurai* were not a landed nobility. There developed a strong solidarity within each village based on distinctions of rank, not of class strata. And rank was achieved then, as it is now, by seniority and communal respect.

The Tokugawa isolation, which lasted until the middle of the nineteenth century, resulted in the preservation of Buddhism and ancestor worship (Shinto) as the exclusive matrices for the religious life of the people. For the *shogunate* successfully repulsed not only armed invasions but the historic thrust of Christianity which was then riding on the crest of European colonialism. After initial successes by Francis Xavier, Christianity was crushed by slaughtering the inhabitants of Shimabara.

"We import technology, not culture nor religion," I was told by Kazuo Nukasawa, assistant director in the *Keidanren* (Federation of Economic Organizations). "The missionaries failed to introduce Christianity into this country and that is one reason for our success," he boasted. "But," he added, "that may also be one of the reasons for our failure to adjust to foreign environments."

Nukasawa's boast-lament reflects the anguish of today's individual Japanese whose irrepressible enterprise has forced him, unprepared, to deal with foreign cultures. His is a sterilized but far from sterile culture. Christianity might have given him what the

Spaniards call *mundo,* the French *savoir faire,* or the Americans just a plain sense of humor. But it might also have shattered the solid homogeneity and upset the delicate balance of his society. And scholars could not now be waxing lyrical over "constructive tribalism" as the secret of Japan's coming industrial supremacy over a Western Christendom debilitated by its own destructive internecine tribalism.

At the heart of the irrepressible tribalism of the Japanese is the *ie,* the family system, which differs radically from its counterparts in China with its traditional patriarchal unity, in India with its stress on sibling relationship, or in Latin Catholic countries with its extension to *compadres, ahijados,* and *padrinos.* Most of these counterparts have been weakened by modernization and urbanization. Not so with the *ie* which has not only survived these processes but has provided the propelling force for their acceleration.

Chie Nakane, the noted Japanese anthropologist, would call *ie* a household group rather than a family. In her remarkable book, *Japanese Society,* she explains this important distinction:

> In my view, the most basic element of the *ie* institution is not that form whereby the eldest son and his wife live together with the old parents nor an authority structure in which the household head holds the power and so on. Rather, the *ie* is a corporate residential group and, in the case of agriculture or other similar enterprises, *ie* is a managing body. The *ie* comprises household members (in most cases the family members of the household head, but others in addition to family members may be included), who thus make up the units of a distinguishable social group. In other words, the *ie* is a social group constructed on the basis of an established frame of residence and often of management organization. What is important here is that the human relationships within this household group are thought of as more important than all other human relationships.[1]

Under this system, the son-in-law who lives in the same household becomes more important than the son who has left to found his own household. Outsiders with not the remotest kinship may be invited to join the household and become heirs or successors, and servants and clerks living in the household are treated as family members. One's neighbor becomes more important than cousins who live far from home. In the words of an old saying, "You can carry on your life without cousins but not without your neighbors."

A sort of democratic, anti-nepotistic situation arises where a wealthy brother is not duty bound to help a poor brother or sister

---

[1]Chie Nakane, *Japanese Society* (London: Penguin, 1973), pp. 4-5. This work contains a detailed analysis of Japanese cultural homogeneity.

who has set up a separate household. Social disparity becomes common among siblings. In the same city, the mayor's brother may be a postman and a businessman's widowed sister may work as a domestic servant in another household. (A similar system prevailed in the early Philippine *balangay* or village settlement, where the chief or *datu*—before the Spaniards came and made his office hereditary—rose to office by consensus and often had a brother who was an ordinary freeman and another who was a slave.)

With kinship de-emphasized, the *ie* is held together by strict enforcement of rank. Status prevails over age and sex. The actual head of the household outranks his retired father. Age is a deciding factor only among those of equal rank. "Japanese women are nearly always ranked as inferiors," says Nakane, "not because their sex is considered inferior but because women seldom hold higher social status."

The decisions within the *ie* are reached by discussion and consensus, not unlike the *musjuwara* in traditional Java, the democratic dimensions of which are only now being found by some observers to bo of potential uoe in tho United Nationo. In tho oarly traditional *io*, all members of the household accepted the opinion of the head without discussion. But in the latter-day *ringi-sei* ("consensus system"), the head does not force his ideas on the members who may freely present their ideas for adoption by the head.

Because the sibling, or horizontal, relationship loses its importance and the stress is on the interaction of different ranks, the *ie* is called a vertical group. Here lie the microcosmic beginnings of the total vertical Japanese society where group is more important than individual and where horizontal occupational guilds do not exist.

In the deliberate, selective modernization conducted since the Meiji restoration, the original structures of the society were not destroyed. They were carefully preserved and utilized in the building of the new state, in the pursuit of the three Meiji objectives of constitutionalism, industrialization, and military organization. In a society saturated with the concept and ethics of *ie*, industrialization began its march in the factories of companies which quite readily and efficiently took on the features of the old village household.

One of these early companies, the Japanese National Railways, was called *Kokutetsu-ikka*, which literally means "one railway family." As part of the modernization effort, the company housed a "union" which would not have come up to the standards of George Meany, the U.S. labor leader, since it incorporated both workers and management and was justified as "management-labor harmony."

Today, a company is thought of as an *ie*. The employer is the head, and the employees are the members of the household. Since he is a member of the household, he is hired for life (or until retirement with a substantial pension) and will not be fired except for disloyalty to the company's ideals. If he is inefficient at one job, the company will find something else for him to do.

The employee is engaged totally (*marugakae*, "completely enveloped"), which means that what is employed is not only the man's labor but the total man. The employer takes responsibility for the employee's family. In exchange, the employee's family must now worry primarily about the company and not about relatives who live in other places. The family ceases to be itself an *ie* but just a family unit of the bigger household or *ie*, namely, the company. In the traditional *ie*, there were comparable family units, those of clerks and servants who belonged to the household.

Even if the employee should want to change companies, he would find it difficult to do so. In the vertical Japanese society, there are no horizontal craft unions, no bonds between workers of the same category, no exchanges of information with fellow workers outside the company. The employee is as isolated as the married-in son-in-law is from his original family.

In any case, the company sees to it that the employee has little reason to want change. He lives in company housing and enjoys hospital insurance, company recreation areas, company gifts on the occasion of births, marriages, or deaths in the family, and all forms of company advice. Since loyalty is more important than efficiency—or better, since loyalty begets efficiency—he will rise on seniority and not merit. The merit system is feasible only in a highly specialized section of a large company or in a relatively new and small private firm. In a big company, a general shift from the seniority to the merit system would, Nakane says, "involve not a partial or technical change in payment or promotion but a drastic reformation of the structure itself, . . . the informal structure within the factory . . . derived from the overall social organization of the country." Such a major change would "invite confusion and conflict."[2]

The actual operation of the company is not, unlike that of Western establishments, governed by the written bylaws of the corporation. The rules and relationships, informally understood but strictly observed, are identical to those of the traditional *ie*. Modern techniques such as mass singing, mass calisthenics, and creed recitations, once used effectively to whip up the fever of militarism, are now utilized to promote the *ie* group consciousness. The workers at Matsushita Electric, the *Economist*'s Norman Macrae writes, "honestly feel only a little silly" as they sing together their daily hymn:

> Let's put our strength and mind together,
> Doing our best to promote production,

---

[2] Nakane, *Japanese Society*, p. 88.

Sending our goods to the people of the world,
Endlessly and continuously,
Like water gushing from a fountain.
Grow, industry, grow, grow, grow!
Harmony and sincerity![3]

In the spring of 1972, I visited the Matsushita Electric plant in Fukuoka where my son, just graduated from Sophia University in Tokyo, was in the midst of an eighteen-month training program during which he learned every phase of the operations, from tightening the screws on electric pencil sharpeners to accounting and management. From the visual evidence, conversations through interpreters, and the personal observations of my son, I could sense that no one felt the least bit silly moving about in their gray uniform shirts and caps (worn by everyone while in the plant, including top management), some with distinctive stripes indicating length of service, like noncommissioned officers. I saw in their faces, if not pride, an air of serene confidence, an absence of insecurity.

My son and daughter-in-law were lodged in a typical Japanese one-level bungalow in a row of company housing (shataku) located a few minutes' drive from the plant in a suburb of the city of Fukuoka. His neighbors were middle-aged, middle-management executives of the company, which was quite a privilege for a young foreign trainee of twenty-three. The special treatment was due to his relationship to Matsushita's Filipino partner in its joint venture in the Philippines, an industrialist whose daughter my son had married after graduation from Sophia University.

The couple enjoyed the rare experience of intimate contact with the inner workings of the informal rules of the ie, something very few foreigners manage to achieve. I had a quick taste of this experience. (Presumably an increasing number of foreigners who manage to live with Japanese families for extended periods while studying or working are able to observe the household ie at work, but the company ie is somewhat more difficult to get close to.)

On the evening of my arrival at my son's home, his neighbor, Hasegawa-san, a general affairs officer of the company with whom my son had established a friendly relationship, paid me a courtesy call with his wife. He brought me a bottle of five-year-old Suntory whiskey, and, with my son as interpreter, we had an enjoyable evening exchanging stories of my imprisonment by the Kempeitai (Japanese military police) and his experiences with the company and taking flash snapshots. It did not seem like a particularly different evening from what I might have experienced had I visited my son in a British company compound.

The difference was, I later learned, that Haegawa-san and his

    [3] Norman Macrae, "Pacific Century, 1975-2075?" *Economist*, January 4, 1975, p. 16.

wife were not in the habit of paying these calls on the other families in the six-family row. Apparently, due to shades of difference in rank (one or two years seniority makes a lot of difference), no intimate house-calling was ever observed on the street. On very special occasions, some intimate but rather stiff contact would occur. If one's son or daughter were about to enter college from middle school, one would visit each neighbor and pass out gifts, like an American father passing out cigars on the birth of a child. If there is a death in the family, it is expected that the neighbors, in spite of shades in rank, will come to offer funeral contributions.

But on holidays (the biggest is New Year's Day), there is no exchanging of gifts in the neighborhood. Instead, people troop to their respective immediate superiors who live in a separate *shataku* to deliver their customary ceremonial gift offerings. The women do engage in typical casual small talk but only in front of the house or across the fence. There is no dropping in for coffee or tea. And invariably each wife is expected to boast (American wives would be expected to lament) that their husbands are consistently working late at the office, for working late is a mark of the man's importance and a confirmation of his and his family's total commitment to the company. A wife is covered with shame if the neighbors should catch her husband coming home before sundown. Working late, by the way, could include spending some time in a downtown bar, another accepted mark of status.

After his training in Fukuoka, my son was named assistant to the vice-president and general manager of the Matsushita operations in Puerto Rico. His new boss spoke no English or Spanish, and my son's command of both plus Japanese made him a useful channel of communication between management and workers. He became personally involved in·the "working late" syndrome. He was also thus directly introduced into the consensus processes of the company *ie*. All those involved in top management in the San Juan operation, except the personnel manager who is Puerto Rican, are Japanese. After office hours, the managers would often meet until the late hours of the night to discuss policy. My son was often asked to attend so that he might communicate and articulate the decisions more accurately to the Puerto Rican personnel, including the personnel manager. "The discussions always seemed interminable," he says, "but in the end everybody seemed satisfied that he had contributed to the decision."

In February, 1975, management-level American personnel of the C. Itoh (one of the Japanese "Big Six") in Texas complained that they were being excluded from the decision-making process by the Japanese management. They were told that the company had been excluding them because policy decisions were made at night and including them would have created family problems since American wives, unlike their Japanese counterparts, are not in the habit of exulting over their husbands' working late.

But if the Japanese seem reluctant to share their consensus with the "natives" at night, they are quite ready to share it fruitfully by day. *Fortune* reported in March, 1975, that American employees in Japanese-run factories (zippers, television, soy sauce) "seem to like" the "rule by consultation" with supervisors down the line helping to formulate policy. But the end of that story is not yet in sight, for it is not clear from the report how far the *ie* group system will succeed in overcoming an important American institution, to which there is no counterpart in Japan, the horizontal craft union.

The Japanese labor unions once a year put on a terrifying act of protest and demand. It is called the Spring Offensive, and the unionists march massively down the streets, snake-dancing and shouting slogans. But the date, the locations, the uniforms, even the slogans, have already been known to the public for months.

"They go around and it looks terrible," Bernard Krisher, *Newsweek's* Tokyo bureau chief told me in January, 1975. "You think that the country is going to hell. But this lasts only one day!" The next day all is settled; the company managers, after months of consultation with government officials on how much of a wage increase the economy can bear, after consulting the computer on how much the company itself can give in, and after quiet consensus talks with union leaders, have just been waiting for the "annual ritual ballet," as Krisher would call it, the one-day strike, to come and go before announcing the acceptable compromise increase.

The Japanese labor movement has become a cooperative member of the national *ie*. It can do no more. It cannot, like American or European unions, present an independent national front, for its members are intracompany and not intercompany in scope and are captive components of the company *ie*.

Tourists in the spring are treated to a unique spectacle in hotels and restaurants. At the Imperial Hotel in Tokyo, if one is lucky enough to register on the right day, one will see all the hotel help, including head waiters, wearing arm bands with such pugnacious slogans as "It's a bad company and we are on strike!" All the while, however, they are serving the customers with the usual smile, bow, and dispatch. For they are only on symbolic strike. Nobody ever really stops working because they expect to work for the Imperial for the rest of their lives, and they will not allow the rival Okura Hotel to profit at the Imperial's expense.

A Maoist delegate at a conference in Tokyo, reports Macrae, witnessed a demonstration in a park and called it "the most exciting thing since Paris in May, 1968." He was shocked to find the next day that it was not headlined in the Tokyo press. Another witness who spoke Japanese understood why. He saw all the demonstrators give their names and the name of their union to the police as they entered the park. Inside the park, "they wound headbands round their forehead, unpacked shields and weapons, made the ritual gestures." Then they packed things away, carefully cleared the litter, and filed out.[4]

This ritualism would seem to explain why, in spite of the high rate of unionized labor, the Japan Socialist party has never been in power. There are 12 million in the entire labor movement. Of these, 4.4 million are government employees, most of whose support goes to the Japan Socialist party; and 2.4 million are from the private sector and usually favor the Democratic Socialist party. Yet, unlike the mass membership of union members in Britain's Socialist party, the Japan Socialist party actually has only 40,000 members and the Democratic Socialists, 20,000. The beneficiary of the ritualism is the Liberal Democratic party which has monopolized power since the Second World War.

Formal Versus Informal

Unlike Oxford or Harvard, Tokyo University (the prewar Imperial University) does not cater to a social elite. Sons of farmers, workers, industrialists, and professors stand on the same footing at the entrance examinations and after graduation form a social clique so effective that Nakane compares them to an Indian caste whose consciousness is, however, "felt more by those outside the group than those inside it." *Todai* (short for Tokyo *Dai Gakku*) graduates monopolize top positions in the big business groups and in government. They provide the unseen "informal" force that binds government and business whose inter-relationship cannot be explained in terms of the traditional norms of a capitalist society.

The formal versus the informal system is perhaps best detected by analyzing the national economic planning system. The formal process begins with the prime minister requesting the Economic Council to draft a plan. The Council is advisory in character and is composed of about thirty members, mostly presidents and board chairmen of big business groups, and former government officials. Membership is honorary, and the members are usually too busy with other duties to think of economic planning.

So the planning passes to the Bureau of Comprehensive Planning of the Economic Planning Agency (EPA), which forms the secretariat of the Economic Council. They produce a national economic plan which is quite elaborate, setting forth areas and targets, estimates of growth, indices, etc. "But the planning targets," says Rutaro Komiya, professor of economics at Tokyo University, "are mere compilations of opinions, and the estimates are about as reliable as a long-term weather forecast spiced with wishful thinking." The national plan, therefore, says Komiya, is not binding since "nobody feels much obligation to observe its figures." There is ritualism

---

[4]Macrae, "Pacific Century," p. 21.

here again for, he observes, references to the national plan "are seldom more than ceremonial."

The real planning is done by the industrial sectors and is decided informally by (1) the *genkyoku*, the coordinating offices and councils on the government side, (2) private industry associations, (3) the *zaikai*, the central businessmen's circles, and (4) the banks. These four sides "traditionally spend long hours of negotiation" to reach consensus "by mutual persuasion, coordination, and sometimes threats."[5]

Government officials usually expect to join the private groups after or even before retirement (the retirement age is fifty-five). In the end, therefore, it is the voice of industry itself that prevails in the consensus. "Japanese governments do not really rule," says Macrae. "They pull on strings whose other ends are not connected to anything."[6] Nakane agrees. The business groups really run the country, and "even the law is powerless to offer any check."[7]

The Fair Trade Commission, designed to undertake antitrust activities like its American counterpart, is allowed to go through the ritual of "breaking up the big groups" every once in a while. Its proposals in 1975, aimed at dismantling interlocking stock schemes, have been tabled by the Diet, whose conservative majority are hoping it will die a "quiet death."

The Bank of Japan, Japan's equivalent of the Federal Reserve Board, supports the entire credit structure. In what the Japanese themselves call the "bicycle economy" where the investor must keep pressing onward lest he topple over, the flow of credit cannot stop, and commercial banks, with the full backing of the Bank of Japan, engage in practices which to the Western observer would certainly lead to disaster. They grant the most audacious loans, normally lending up to 95 percent of their deposits and sometimes in excess of their deposits, overlending to an already overborrowed industry.

The Japanese dependence on foreign raw materials explains the "bicycle" overinvestment. "They must pre-empt tomorrow's market," said Professor Ballon in an interview. "Their investment could never be justified in present terms, but tomorrow's." When the Ministry of International Trade and Industry allocates resources, it bases itself on tomorrow's market and today's capacity for expansion. This is why Japanese industry for twenty years has been investing between 30 and 40 percent of its GNP, twice the rate in Western nations. Japanese corporations are capitalized on 80 percent or more in borrowings and the rest in equity. "To the West that means bankruptcy," Ballon pointed out to me, "but the point is

---

[5]Ryutaro Komiya, "Economy Planning in Japan," *Challenge* 18 (May/June 1975): 14.

[6]Macrae, "Pacific Century," p. 21.

[7]Nakane, *Japanese Society*, p. 156.

that Japanese corporations, 'bankrupt' for the last twenty years, have been very successful!" He suggests that the question should not be "what is wrong with the Japanese corporations but what is wrong with the Western definition of bankruptcy." A company's financial report makes no sense unless one knows what other companies it is related to. "They've got an interlocking system of financing their industries," said *Far Eastern Economic Review* editor Derek Davies in an interview, "which means an individual firm is not going to go bust. A firm in America will go bust because there is no one supporting it except the bank which forecloses, as in Britain."

Here, then, for the first time in history, we have a nation which appears to be an almost flawless unit. Former Prime Minister Hayato Ikeda once compared it to a ship in which "the government is the captain and the *zaikai* the compass." The people, of course, are the crew. To shift the metaphor, it is a locomotive on a monorail. The irreducible forward action necessary to prevent disaster enables it to leap overseas and operate almost anywhere at will, in giant former enemies like the United States, the Soviet Union, and now China; or smaller developing territories, communist or capitalist, like North Vietnam and Indonesia. It is the Tokyo Express, and it appears to be on a collision course with Southeast Asia.

IV

Rebels and Dropouts

There *are* Japanese who rebel against the vertical *ie*. But when they jump off the "bicycle action," they cause violence—at home and, unfortunately, abroad. These anti-*ie* rebels are not to be confused with American antiestablishment protestors, from whom they differ in motivation, tactics, and extent of scruples.

The American protest movement draws from all walks of life, many times recruiting from among those who need no further status or wealth to make it. Some may, in fact, be bored with the prospect of not having to struggle to survive or to rise. The Japanese rebel is more often one who did not make it. He is surprisingly young for one of that category, but in Japan the verdict of society, determining whether one is to stay on the escalator which proceeds to the top or to get off to take the stairs that end halfway up in mediocrity, comes at a very early age, more precisely at the point at which the results of university entrance examinations are announced.

We have seen how the Todai Club, that informal clique of graduates of the University of Tokyo, dominates Japanese business and government. "Top-ranking companies limit applications to the new graduates of top-ranking universities," says Chie Nakane. "There is more intense competition between and a more strictly defined hierarchical order among universities [because] with the rise of economic standards there is an increase in the number of those able to go to university." "The chances of entry into a top-ranking university," adds Nakane, "are enhanced if one applies from a high school of repute and so on down to primary school."[1]

This explains the insistence of the Japanese government on maintaining Japanese schools abroad for the children of their

---

[1]Nakane, *Japanese Society*, pp. 117-18.

businessmen and diplomats which will conform with the standards of the rigid system at home. One of the targets of protest of the Chulalongkorn University students was the "privileged school" exclusively for Japanese students which, unlike other private schools, was not under the control of the Thai government. Similar schools are found in Indonesia.

Some Japanese mothers, says *Newsweek*'s Bernard Krisher, are not even satisfied with these overseas schools. "They are so concerned that their children follow the day-by-day curriculum required by the education ministry in Tokyo so that they can get into the right colleges." The curriculum leaves very little time for foreign languages, foreign customs, or mixing with foreign children. Sometimes, discontented mothers go back to Japan with their children to place them in better schools, and the fathers are left alone, creating temporarily broken families that present problems to the local Japanese manager who "must make sure his men don't get too serious in their affairs with the local prostitutes."

Wives are apparently ready to take chances in leaving their husbands to make sure their children are on equal terms with those who do not have to go abroad. Don Oberdofer of the *Washington Post* reported from Tokyo in August, 1975, that "pressures to succeed have become so immense that many parents coach their children in preschool days to win admission to the best primary schools, which are considered the pathway to the best secondary schools and thus training grounds for the best universities." He referred to a recent survey by Sanwa Bank which showed that "about one-fifth of all elementary and junior high school students in large cities are being tutored individually or in groups after school hours, and another two-fifths are taking non-academic courses. . . ."

Oberdofer interviewed a typical Japanese father and mother caught in the system who "believe such educational stress is neither healthy nor necessary [since] the children are no longer enjoying a childhood of exploring and inquiring but becoming drudges and highly trained instruments for automatic response."

In August, 1974, terrorists bombed the Mitsubishi headquarters in Tokyo, killing 8 people and injuring more than 300 others. In the next nine months, the offices of ten more companies were bombed, injuring 32 people.

Most of the young men arrested for the bombings "had done well in high school but failed to capture the prize of entry into a prestigious university," writes Jonathan Rollow of the *Washington Post*. Most of Japan's "long-term drifters [are] high school graduates who have failed to pass the university entry examinations. . . . [That failure] is a blow to family pride and to the individual student's hopes for a future career." Having failed once, they can try again and sometimes "spend a year or two preparing for another set of entry exams, either at home or in one of the special preparatory schools, which in Tokyo alone cram knowledge into 13,000 students a year." But most of the first failures either end up in second-rate universities, drop out of the "education rat race," or commit suicide.

According to one Japanese psychology professor, some of them turn to terrorism because they are frustrated by the system and tend to become sensitive to discrimination in general. The terrorists place no limit on the venting of their frustrations at home. In August, 1975, five members of the Japanese Red Army seized the American consulate in Kuala Lumpur and by holding fifty hostages, including the American consul, succeeded in forcing the release of five of their imprisoned comrades in Tokyo, with whom they were flown to Libya. In 1972, Red Army terrorists massacred twenty-six people, most of them pilgrims from Puerto Rico, in an attack on Tel Aviv airport. In 1973, they hijacked a Japan Air Lines plane to North Korea. In 1974, they attacked an oil refinery in Singapore and seized the French ambassador to the Netherlands.

Both the system and those who rebel against it would seem to be breeding violence. Caught in the dilemma are those who attempt a compromise "nonviolent dropout," by getting off the Tokyo Express and getting on a hand trolley, hitching the trolley to the train in hope of enjoying the best of both worlds.

Some Japanese assigned to Thailand, for instance, have apparently found a way to achieve this compromise. After their tour of duty is over, they leave the company so they do not have to go home. Because they remain Japanese citizens and because they have accumulated experience, they are of value to Japanese business, and they manage to enter into independent contracts either with their old company or with another Japanese company. Under these arrangements, they do not enjoy the lifetime security of the ordinary company personnel. But they are willing to give that up for very practical reasons.

"As long as they belong to the vertical structure," Tokyo anthropologist T. Aoki told me, "they have to go back home after a three- or four-year cycle. When they get back to Japan there is no hope at all because, at age twenty-six or twenty-seven, single men in Tokyo get a monthly salary of $300, whereas in Bangkok they get about $1000 and enjoy very special status because they can hire maids and stay in very nice mansions. In Tokyo they have to live in a very small place."

Sometimes they marry Thai women, but even then they "maintain Japanese conduct [while enjoying] the living standard and special status of a foreigner." This special breed of dropouts is apparently "looked down upon" by the company regulars because of their ambivalence and opportunism, for while they "stick close together and always criticize the policies of Japanese companies" they in fact continue to depend on the companies for their livelihood. They are "kind of medium people, the in-between people," said Aoki, "and they are getting larger in number every year."

Harvard Business School's Michael Yoshino confirmed the existence of these dropouts in Thailand but felt there were only "maybe a dozen" (in 1974, there were 1,306 permanent Japanese residents in Thailand; assuming an average family of five, a dozen dropout families would total sixty or 4 percent of the permanent Japanese population). But he agreed with Aoki that even these numbers were a symptom of the increasing impatience of some Japanese over the difficult, dull, and mechanical upward mobility in their society. Some people, said Aoki, "are rapidly losing their hopes for the future, [and] working for the company is losing its clarity of purpose." Life in Tokyo "is very flat, [the people] want to be rich . . . but they live in a vacuum." Aoki seemed to feel that the ie-group was failing to fill that vacuum, and more people were beginning to look for the solution outside the group.

Dropping out of the system while still depending on it may solve the personal problems of alienation of some Japanese, but it does not cure the offensive exclusivism of the ie presence abroad, since the compromisers inevitably form their own group somewhat peripheral to but still very much a part of the vertical system.

Furthermore, pressures within the system that cause the dropouts could suddenly produce unprogrammed eruptions. The feeling among an increasing number of the younger generation of being hemmed in by the rigid vertical structure is related to the physical limitations of Japan itself. The refusal of the dropouts in Thailand to leave their "mansions" for "a very small place" in Tokyo is, as Aoki indicates, a symptom of a growing disillusionment and even despair among younger Japanese about their future. I found the problem of land insistently impressed upon me by Japanese of all persuasions. Former Domei labor union head Minoru Takita lashed out at "irresponsible futurologists who overlook the fact that Japan holds only 0.25 percent of the land of the earth while its overall GNP is 11 percent." Takita warns that "Japan is already overdense and nature here has been destroyed." "Because of the scarcity of flat land," observes Yoshino, "the three industrial areas—those around greater Tokyo, Osaka, and Ise Bay—make up less than a third of Japan's land area; yet in 1974 they had more than half her population, produced nearly three-quarters of her manufactures, and consumed 64 percent of her energy."

Masao Kunihiro, a teacher of cultural anthropology and international relations, spoke of a survey he had conducted among his students at Sophia University who were in their early twenties. Of them, 72 percent stated that "they have no hope whatsoever of owning a tiny little bit of land on which to build a tiny little house between the time of their graduation and their compulsory retiring age of fifty-five. . . . These are well-educated kids," Kunihiro stressed, "not potential arsonists or rapists—yet 72 percent of them say that they have no hope whatsoever." He predicted that "their agony, their frustrations will not long be pent up [but] in due course" might find violent expression. "Economic problems like these will give rise to social unrest and political instability," he adds, "so I simply cannot subscribe to the optimistic prognostications about the future of Japan."

Professor Hiroharu Seki, a political scientist at Tokyo University, believes that land, in fact, is the key to the industrial future of Japan. "If the rise in land prices is stopped and construction costs are lowered," he envisions a coming flourishing "period of housing industry." Anyone who has been inside the cramped, wood-and-paper, albeit tastefully appointed, quarters of even the more prosperous businessmen in Tokyo will appreciate the potential for a construction industry stimulated by lowered land prices. It would satisfy a national hunger for adequate housing, "just like the auto industry in the United States," Seki recalls, met the commuting demands of suburban America.

The secret formula for reversing or even arresting upward trends in land prices in a capitalist society has not yet been discovered. If there is one awaiting discovery, the resilient vertical society may be the first to find it. If it does and the construction industry is spurred, the housing will perforce, and perhaps symbolically, rise vertically. But it will be more than a symbolic achievement. For once again the traditional system will have outrun any revolution, and the Tokyo Express will have been kept on course.

V

Collision Course

Communication

In January, 1974, the first two collisions of the Tokyo Express occurred in Bangkok and Jakarta. In the post mortem analyses of the two, the Japanese themselves admit that the problem of communication is primary among the causes.

Language, of course, is the first obvious obstacle. The Japanese have suddenly become manufacturers, traders, and lenders to the world without knowing much of the current *lingua franca* (English) or the local languages. Yet, this is an obstacle which determined Japanese could, with some intensive training, readily overcome.

But the problem of communication goes deeper than the question of language, for Japanese have difficulty communicating even when they do speak English or the local language. In fact, they have difficulty communicating with each other in their own language. These difficulties are another characteristic of the vertical *ie*, which in its pristine form follows the Japanese wherever they go.

Before the calling card was invented, life must have been a sustained trauma for the Japanese who had to make new acquaintances every day in the course of his business. The crucial role of the calling card in the daily life of the Japanese is described by anthropologist Chie Nakane, and her description is worth reproducing in full:

> The ranking order within a given institution affects not only the members of that institution but through them it affects the establishment of relations between persons from different institutions when they meet for the first time. On such occasions the first thing that the Japanese do is exchange name cards. The act has crucial social implications. Not only do name cards give information about the name (and the characters with which it is written) and the address; their

more important function is to make clear the title, the position and the institution of the person who dispenses them. It is considered proper etiquette for a man to read carefully what is printed on the card, and to adjust his behavior, mode of address and so on in accordance with the information it gives him. By exchanging cards, both parties can gauge the relationship between them in terms of relative rank, locating each other within the known order of their society. Only after this is done are they able to speak with assurance, since, before they can do so, they must be sure of the degree of honorific content and politeness they must put into their words.[1]

I have traveled in trains and planes in Japan many times and I have never seen a Japanese casually make the acquaintance of the man next to him. What used to be a joke about Englishmen and formality is a real institution in Japan. The man next to you is not of your *ie* so why bother to talk to him? Besides, since you will probably never get to the card-exchanging stage, how do you know what his rank is and what language and demeanor to use with him? Is he your *sempai* ("senior") or *kohai* ("junior")? He could even be your *doryo* ("colleague"), but can you tell his age or year of graduation from school or college? Will you call him Watanabe-san, Watanabe-kun or just plain Watanabe, assuming he gets to tell you his name is Watanabe?

A study by two Yale University graduate students, Ernesto Ordoñez, a Filipino, and Kanoh Wada, a Japanese, evaluated the impact of socio-cultural norms on the effectiveness of T-group learning in Japan, using as subjects forty-eight staff members of the Shell Oil Company of Japan. The study found that the Japanese seniority system was a "strong barrier [to] openness and trust, expression of feelings, or giving and receiving constructive feedbacks." Under such conditions, the study says, quoting the social scientist, Chris Argyris, "people will tend to play it safe and be cautious rather than take risks related to emotionally laden topics; frustrations will be high but not dealt with because feelings are not admissible."[2]

The study cites twelve different ways in which a Japanese can say "I" and at least five different suffixes for an individual's name. "Failure of the appropriately classified usage of these titles will be generally regarded as a challenge to the maintenance of *face*." "Face" is important to the Japanese, and he is careful not to lose it nor to cause the other person to lose it. When a Japanese fails to carry out a promise or a request, he utters a remark which is directly

[1]Nakane, *Japanese Society*, pp. 31-2.

[2]Ernesto Ordoñez and Kanoh Wada, "The Impact of Socio-Cultural Norms on the Effectiveness of T-Group Learning in Japan," Yale University graduate thesis, 1970.

translated, "I have no face to see you." A plain "no" is the height of discourtesy in any situation, since flat denials "are considered to be injurious to the maintenance of the other person's face." All this creates "social distance" which insures that "human behavior and the expression of one's inner feelings will be significantly influenced and controlled by the ritual elements."

The ritualism of the *ie* makes it necessary for a Japanese to acquire a special talent to cross freely the boundary to another Japanese community. One can imagine the talent it takes for him to cross to a foreign community or for him to receive a foreigner into his community. A stranger must be accepted not only by him but by the group, and even upon acceptance he is regarded as of peripheral or lower status but not equal.

It is against this background that one should regard a Japanese as he deals with Southeast Asians, engaging them in apparently indecisive dialogue and shunning socialization that he regards as both difficult and unnecessary.

"The Japanese are too exclusive," Indonesia's Vice President Sultan Hamengkubowono has said, "They don't mix with our people. It's always business. They have their own club, their own restaurant, their school. It brings bad memories of the occupation."

"I have many friends from many countries—but where are my Japanese friends?" asks a Bandung (Java) University professor. "They are industrialists, not humanists."

"If an American company offered me Rp (rupiah) 150,000 and a Japanese company Rp200,000," hypothesized an Indonesian textile engineer, "I wouldn't hesitate even for a moment to work for the American firm because of the way I would be treated. Americans at least make you *feel* they don't discriminate against you. You can walk in and talk to the top manager on an equal basis."

"They are Japanese in the beginning, Japanese in the end, and in between it's all Japanese," complained Ali Noorluddin, head of the Japan Committee of the Chamber of Commerce of Indonesia, whom I visited at his office. The committee was set up at the suggestion of the Keidanren (Federation of Economic Organizations) officials with whom he had met in Tokyo. "But it is still a one-way street," he said.

"Even on the golf course they play only with company colleagues," an Indonesian major general who had been stationed in Manila complained to me.

In Thailand, where the Japanese presence has been imposing, Bunchana Atthakor, just before leaving the post of minister of commerce under the military dictatorship in 1973, made a celebrated speech in which he denounced the Japanese who "come in Japanese planes, ride in Japanese tour buses with Japanese guides, stay in Japanese hotels, eat in Japanese restaurants and go to Japanese nightclubs." After the fall of the dictatorship, the press, never really effectively censored by the triumvirate, broke out into more lively and imaginative attacks. On the day Prime Minister Kakuei Tanaka was to land for his ill-fated official visit in January, 1974, the Thai English-language daily, the *Nation*, published its own fanciful version of what his schedule would be if he came as an ordinary Japanese tourist. Of course everything was Japanese from the airplane to the Japanese-backed movie to discussion topics over dinner. An excerpt shows the strain of bitterness in the article.

January 10

05:00—Awaken by a Seiko alarm clock, a compliment from Muang Thong Company. Morning toilet with Japanese toiletries, compliments from Saba Pattana Pibul Company. Golf at Japanese Alumni Association.

08:00—A meeting with Chairman of Siam Motors Company, the import of old Datsun cars for sale in Thailand is the major topic.

12:00—Lunch at Daikoku.

14:00—A movie at Siam Theatre showing "The 20,000 Mile Chase," a production from Japanese investment.

Back to Amarin Hotel in a Subaru car provided by Pithan Company.

16:00—Meeting with Mr. Chaw Chawkhuanyuen on the Kra Canal Project.

17:00—Wreath laying at Phra Pinklao Bridge in congratulation to the Japanese firm which succeeded in deceiving Thailand into building the bridge.

Travel in a Mazda provided by Kamolsukosol Company.

19:00—A dinner hosted by Mr. Boonsu Lodchanasathienpap. Discussion topic during the dinner will centre on credit import of Japanese goods and hoarding of the goods for profiteering. . . .[3]

In Honolulu, Japanese group exclusivism is re-enacted daily in the Japanese-owned hotels, shops, restaurants, and tour buses along Waikiki Beach; and the consequent cycling of the money back to Japan is, as in Thailand, a consistent target of criticism. I was told there that "the most critical" issue was the rate at which the

---

[3]"If Tanaka Came as a Japanese Tourist," *Nation* (English-language daily, Bangkok), January 9, 1974.

Japanese were buying up golf courses or building new ones for their exclusive use.

Yet, elsewhere in the United States, the Japanese appear to be making an effort to adjust to the local culture and to cross the communication barrier. In a March, 1975, *Fortune* article, instances are mentioned of Japanese executives, like Katsuo Goto, treasurer of Mitsubishi Aircraft's operation in Texas, who have made the breakthrough. "I've learned to say 'no' instead of 'that's very difficult,' " Goto is quoted as bragging. This bold defiance of "face" creates problems with the home office in Japan, "where Goto's acquired habit of saying 'no' shocks associates."

The article optimistically pictures the American employees as responding well to Japanese management techniques and liking "the sense of participation." In this light, the complaint mentioned earlier, filed by American middle-level executives against exclusion from the decision-making process in C. Itoh in Texas, would appear to be an isolated case and applicable to the top policy decisions only. *Fortune* quotes an American manager at Sony's television plant in San Diego as observing, "It helps that everyone agrees before things are done. You don't have the power struggles and infighting common in many U.S. companies."

But on American territory with a different cultural character, the Japanese do not seem eager to make this accommodation. Conversations with the Japanese managers of the Matsushita operation in Puerto Rico showed they had little confidence in the capacities and potential of the native Puerto Rican.

Where the Japanese have a choice, they have shown a marked preference for the employment of those of Japanese ancestry. Yasumasa Kuroda, a Japanese-American professor of political science at the University of Hawaii and the only one I encountered in my trip across the Pacific who openly used the term "economic animal" in referring to the Japanese ("they sell transistors but they are not interested in what will be broadcast"), stated that empirical data supported the charge that Japanese firms in Hawaii were averse to hiring local minorities. He referred to one of the conclusions of a report on Japanese foreign investment in Hawaii: "Japanese firms in Hawaii employ 18 percent Japanese nationals and 70 percent Japanese-Americans, leading to a strong underrepresentation of persons of Hawaiian, Filipino, Polynesian and Micronesian ancestry."[4]

The barriers erected by the we-versus-they group consciousness of the *ie* would appear to be much higher when "they" belong to a race not historically regarded as the equal of the Japanese. The readiness of the Mitsubishi man in Texas to learn the

---

[4]Robert and Emily Heller, *The Economic and Social Impact of Foreign Investment in Hawaii* (Honolulu: University of Hawaii Economic Research Center, 1973).

American habit of saying "no" might be explained by his consciousness that he is dealing after all with people that only thirty years ago were efficient enough to defeat his country in war. The Japanese may regard Caucasians as a whole as their equal, but there appears to be a tendency to look up to Americans in particular.

Anthropologist Masao Kunihiro, who enjoys the confidence of Prime Minister Takeo Miki, recalls in an interesting article on language barriers that "former Prime Minister Sato stated at a press conference before departing for the United States [at the time when the U.S.-Japan textile negotiations were bogged down]: 'Since Mr. Nixon and I are old friends, the negotiations will be three parts talk and seven parts *haragei*.' The words are difficult to translate into English, for the art of *haragei* is a communication technique peculiar to the Japanese. In a Japanese-English dictionary it is translated as 'belly art; abdominal performance.' The former sounds erotic and the latter like some kind of acrobatic stunt, and neither is what Sato meant. In this word there is a feeling of community of emotions—a desire to be given special consideration since the other fellow is supposed to be your friend, a member of your group. One can understand why Mr. Sato assumed that it would, naturally, be possible to communicate with Mr. Nixon with *haragei*, considering how close the relationship was between them."

Americans, then, are considered to be "of the group" and fairly high in the vertical *ie*. "The tendency of the Japanese to regard international relations as an extension of hierarchic interpersonal relations at home is another durable characteristic," says Kunihiro, adding that Japan "will continue to regard the United States as its superior on the totem pole. . . ."[5]

A survey by Tokyo's Sophia University in June, 1972, showed that 50.2 percent of Japanese feel closer to the United States and Europe than to Asian countries, while only 22.2 percent felt the opposite. In the same vein, Kunihiro said when I interviewed him in Tokyo that he "could not be optimistic about the future of Japan's external relationships within the Southeast Asian countries [because] there is an element of chauvinism, big power chauvinism, involved." He lamented, "I have to admit that I am ashamed of it but I have to admit it." Professor Toru Yano, of Kyoto University, who was in the advance party for the Tanaka visit to Southeast Asia, recalled for me a famous Japanese philosopher who as early as 1894 propounded the Escape-from-Asia theory. Of course, that was before the raw materials and cheap labor of the region became irresistible to developing Japanese industry. "Asia is corrupted," it was argued, "and if Japan tries to go along with Asian people, the Japanese will

---

[5]Masao Kunihiro, "Indigenous Barriers to Communication," *The Wheel Extended* (Toyota quarterly review) 8 (Spring 1974): 16.

get corrupted themselves—so let Japan look rather to the civilized Western nations."

Umarjadi Nyotowijono, a former ambassador and now head of the ASEAN office of the Indonesian Department of Foreign Affairs, studied for fourteen years in Japan (1936-50) and is married to a Japanese. But he told me in Jakarta that he thought "Europeans understand Asians better" than the Japanese do and that "Japanese look down on Indonesians."

A sampling of student opinion at Chulalongkorn University in Bangkok in June, 1974, reflected the thinking that the Japanese "are not generous and look down on Thais and Asians as a whole." The Chinese seem to fare better in Japanese estimation. In a March 4, 1973, *Washington Post* article, Asian specialist Selig Harrison quoted Mohammad Sadli as saying when he was head of the Indonesia investment office in 1973, "It's not just that [the Japanese] think they have a lot to gain from China. The point is that they don't look down on the Chinese as they do on most other Asians. The Japanese and Chinese have deep feelings of cultural affinity and they are natural allies."

In January, 1975, Sadli, then minister of mines, was more cautious when I talked to him in Jakarta. "Maybe we should not generalize," he said and suggested that it might not be racial or cultural considerations but the "business acumen" of the overseas Chinese that made them favorite business partners of the Japanese in Indonesia.

In late 1974 and early 1975, the Tokyo Express suffered two minor but significant collisions, one in Bangkok, the other in Hong Kong. They illustrate complicated problems in cross-cultural communication. In January, 1975, an announcement was made that the Japanese consortium led by Mitsubishi Trading Company was abandoning the HK$5 billion underground railway project thirteen months after its bid had been officially accepted by the Hong Kong government. The colony's governing council was in an uproar. Three months before, another consortium led by Mitsubishi and Mitsui had withdrawn from a commitment to undertake a multibillion *baht* petrochemical project in Thailand.

In Hong Kong the consortium was reported to have used the oil crisis as a reason for its alleged inability to implement the bid. This was being branded a "pretext" in the press, which pointed out that the bid had been submitted after the oil crisis had commenced. The Hong Kong government was threatening to sue for US$33 million and to take reprisals against the more than fifty consortium members with business interests in the colony. In Thailand, the initial formal excuse was a student protest against pollution. After the Thai government had clarified that the project would use the "diaphragm" system which does not use mercury (the cause of Minamata disease), the consortium flatly declared that the project was "uneconomically feasible" [sic] and that "it is more economical for Thailand to import petrochemical products from Japan than to establish an industrial complex for these products here."

Deja Boonchuchuy, an official of the Thai Board of Investments, felt that the consortium's sudden withdrawal was a delaying tactic. Yasuyuki Matsuo, head of the Japan Trade Center in Bangkok, argued that there were five solid reasons for the withdrawal: (1) the oil crisis, (2) the consequent high price of oil products, (3) the decrease in demand for oil products, (4) the tight money policy in Japan (which has since been relaxed), and (5) the opposition of Thai opinion leaders who called it a "death factory." Shortly after the withdrawal, a fairly elaborate exhibition entitled "Polluted Japan" was held under the auspices of the Natural and Environmental Conservation Groups of Thammasat, Chulalongkorn, and Ramkhamhaeng universities.

What remained totally unexplored in both the Hong Kong and Thailand incidents was the reason behind the evident aplomb with which the Japanese withdrew from a written contract, since they are otherwise careful not to lose "face" by failing to carry out a mission or promise. Suicide, in fact, has been the historical prescription for extreme loss of "face" in Japan.

At the root of this apparent contradiction is the ritualism of the Japanese language. Kunihiro says, in the article on language barriers quoted earlier, that there is among the Japanese a "contempt for language." For them, language "is only one means of communication, not the means of communication" as in the West. With the possible exception of pantomime like Marcel Marceau's, it is not possible to understand Western theatre without understanding the dialogue. But, Kunihiro continues, "even in the highly stylized theatrical art forms of Japan, which are far removed from realism, it is possible to follow the plot without the words."

For the Japanese, Kunihiro goes on, "the use of words becomes a sort of ritual, not often to be taken at its face value." Consequently, "it is still quite common to have unwritten contracts between large manufacturers and trading firms [which] seem to exist only for the purpose of specifying stipulations that are an exception to the rule" and often contain in the end a very useful escape clause such as, "All other problems will be settled through consultation."

Kunihiro, who teaches at the Jesuit Sophia University and displays, perhaps, his exposure to scholasticism, calls this Japanese attitude a " 'natural-law' view of things" and concludes that "the contract is just a lot of words; the reality exists somewhere apart from it."[6] Sophia University Professor Ballon confirmed this in an interview: "What the Japanese say and what the Japanese feel are two

---

[6]Kunihiro, "Indigenous Barriers," p. 15.

different things, always. To them what counts is what they feel and not what is being conceptualized. Our problem is that we take the words for what they mean which no Japanese has ever done."

To Ballon, this does not mean an absence of ethical standards among the Japanese but only that "they are less vocal about ethical standards than we are." He said, "Once you have a commitment out of a Japanese, you have it—contract or no contract." He recognizes that the problem arises when there is a contract, for "the Japanese do not react to a piece of paper the way Westerners do." While he does not excuse the Japanese, he sees the need for some "open-mindedness on our part to see that there may be different ways to look at an obligation."

The historical beginnings of the modern concept of obligations arising from contracts came from Roman law principles, one of them being that of *do ut des*, i.e., I give so that you may give. After the giving is done both ways, the obligation and the contractual relationship are finished. This is a concept that appears to be alien to Japanese history and mentality. To the Japanese, personal commitment arises from a mutuality of interests which breeds loyalty. The mutuality has historically been viewed as a vertical, not a horizontal, reality. The basis, in fact, of the structural principle of Japanese society is the relationship between two individuals of upper and lower ranks. The traditional terms which express this relationship are *oyabun* (one with the status of *oya* or "parent") and *kobun* (one with the status of *ko* or "child"). These terms were originally applied to patron and client, landowner and tenant, master and disciple. Today, most Japanese, whatever their occupation or rank, are involved in *oyabun-kobun* relationships. Even top politicians must visit their *oyabun* for final advice before making an important decision.

"The persistence of these native values, manifested ever since the feudal age in the relationship between lord and subject," says Nakane, is the reason for the failure in Japan of the modern contract system which developed in the West. "Plurality of lords" was permissible in the West, thus permitting the development of the modern contract. In Japan, this was not countenanced; personal commitments were considered of lifetime permanence "embodying an ideology far divorced from any sense of contract." Thus, today, "it is difficult for a Japanese to establish operational contractual relations."[7]

The Japanese notion that order in society is attained by vertical commitments and arrangements and not by horizontal contractual relations is reflected even in the apocalyptic vision of top Japanese technocrats. In 1970, Saburo Ohkita, the famed Japanese economic

---

[7]Nakane, *Japanese Society*, p. 82.

planner, told me of his vision of an orderly advance of Japan in this decade. America will make the big computers and the big cars. Japan will make the small computers and small cars. Japan will also abdicate the labor-intensive industries like transistorized electronics to semi-industrialized states with lower labor costs, like South Korea and Taiwan. I wondered where this would leave the pre-industrial Asian nations.

In January, 1975, Ohkita told me he felt his vertical vision, "prediction, not planning," was apparently coming true with the co-operation of market forces. He pointed out that in 1974 Japan's import of textiles from developing nations had reached $1 billion or 170 times the $6-million level attained in 1965, that Hong Kong was already exporting more transistor radios to the United States than Japan was, and that Taiwan may soon be exceeding Japan in the export of television sets.

He admitted that there was now a phase of this vision in progress which he had not specified to me in 1970. Japan was now exporting her heavy industry, due to the problems of pollution and high labor costs at home. The petrochemical project in Thailand was to have been a part of this phase.

Whether planning or prediction, the fidelity of this vision of international development to the vertical quality of harmony in the *ie* is too striking to be mere coincidence. Some independent-minded Japanese leaders have openly criticized it. Kazuji Nagasu, a university professor who was recently elected governor of Kanagawa Prefecture and who in 1974 wrote a significant attack on Japanese overseas policy, singles out this "vertical division of labor" as one of the "ugly features" of Japanese policy in Southeast Asia.[8] He said in a Tokyo interview that he thought all Japanese trade, investment, and *aid* (the emphasis is his) policies were tailored to fit this vertical division and that the "domestic Tokyo-centered regional development strategy" was being extended overseas as "a Japan-centered foreign aid program. . . . What is rotten at home will also be rotten when extended overseas," he said.

Nagasu's strong words are in fact a call to rebellion against the perpetuation of the *ie* culture. There appear to be no signs that such a rebellion is brewing. But this view, coming from the governor of one of the most important prefectures in Japan, re-enforces the feeling that within the framework of the international *ie*, Japan simply looks down on Southeast Asians as, to borrow the folk Americanism of Kunihiro, the bottom of the totem pole. What the Japanese would then instinctively expect from their relations with Southeast Asians is a "lifetime" vertical commitment in which Japan would be the

---

[8]Kazuji Nagasu, "The Super-Illusions of an Economic Superpower," *Japan Interpreter*, Summer/Autumn 1974, p. 153.

oyabun and Southeast Asia the *kobun* and where there is really no place for those horizontal contractual ethics which colonies like Hong Kong, former colonies like Indonesia, and former economic vassals like Thailand appear to have absorbed from the West. Hence, the facility with which the Japanese might disregard the letter of written contracts, for not only are the words in them "meaningless," but as *oyabun* the Japanese may feel entitled to regard every arrangement with *kobun* in light of the *oyabun*'s view of the vertical common welfare. Here would seem to lie the most explosive aspect of the communication crisis.

No Room — Especially at the Top

In the vertical vision of the Japanese investor, there is no room at the top for the local partner. "When the Indonesian partner insists on representation," says an Indonesian technocrat, Yusuf Panglaykim, he is "generally given the position of director of general affairs or personnel."[9] This usually seems to be the rule in areas where the local population has been considered to be at the bottom of the *ie*. Dr. Kien Theeravit, who is the director of the Information Center in the political science department at Chulalongkorn University, complains that in Thailand the Japanese give only "some ceremonial posts and personnel direction to the local Thais."[10] As we have seen, the only Puerto Rican in management at the Matsushita factory in San Juan is the personnel director.

Michael Yoshino's 1974 Harvard Business School study of a sample of twenty-five Japanese subsidiaries in Thailand reveals that the number of Japanese managers in each company ranged from nine to thirty-four with an average of sixteen. "The numbers are significant," stated Yoshino, "in view of the limited size of the operations. There were only three firms in the sample which had more than one thousand employees." The companies sampled were engaged in a wide range of fields, including metal fabrication, synthetic fibers, home appliances, consumer electronics, automobiles, and chemicals and related products. The criteria for selection were: "(1) they were among the largest in a given industry in terms of sales and investment; (2) they had had at least three years of operating experience; and (3) their Japanese parent company had an active role in the management of subsidiaries." The conclusions were further verified in similar subsidiaries in Malaysia and Taiwan. The "heavy use of Japanese managers" was found to be a "major source of tension."

---

[9]Yusuf Panglaykim, *Business Relations Between Indonesia and Japan* (Jakarta: Centre for Strategic and International Studies, 1974), pp. 41-2.

[10]Kien Theeravit, *The Japanese-Thai Economic Interaction as of October 1973* (Bangkok: Chulalongkorn University, 1974), p. 367. Portions of this book are reprinted in the appendix.

Among the 100 percent-owned subsidiaries of the big trading companies engaged in general trading, the ratio of Japanese personnel to local employees is even higher. Table 13 illustrates this point. The fact that the subsidiaries are engaged in the more inti-

Table 13

The Multinational Commercial Presence
of the Ten Leading Trading Companies*
March 31, 1973

	Branches	100%-owned subsidiaries	Subunits or branches	Parent company personnel employed	Local personnel employed
MITSUBISHI	14	23	82	763	2,460
MITSUI	15	20	79	802	2,133
MARUBENI	15	17	65	592	2,041
C. ITOH	8	11	90	584	1,500
NISSHO-IWAI	5	12	87	560	1,120
SUMITOMO	8	10	68	476	973
TOMEN	9	11	55	334	632
NICHIMEN	9	12	46	306	572
KANEMATSU-GOSHO	6	9	44	330	850
ATAKA	6	7	50	234	407

*These entities include only those established for general trading.

Source: Michael Yoshino

mate function of trading may account for the high percentage of Japanese personnel, in some cases higher than 50 percent. But even if the percentage in the manufacturing subsidiaries in Thailand sampled is lower (see Table 14), the managerial post most available to local executives is that of personnel manager, even though in a substantial number of cases the positions of chairman of the board and president may be left to the local partner (although, under the "package deal," these could be ceremonial).

Substantially contrasting figures are shown in Table 15, compiled from a 1975 survey of U.S. firms in Thailand and Indonesia by Business International Corporation of New York. This table shows that U.S. firms hire more local managers than do Japanese firms. The exceptions are the top positions of chairman and president. The high rate of Americans occupying these two top positions could be

Table 14

The Extent to Which Japanese Managers Held Key Positions in Twenty-five Japanese Manufacturing Subsidiaries in Thailand, 1973

Position	Percent of Subsidiaries in Which Japanese Nationals Occupied a Position
Chairman of the Board	31.5%
President	56.5
Executive vice president	61.2
Accounting manager	87.0
Production manager	85.6
Marketing manager	80.2
Personnel manager	51.3
General affairs manager	61.7

Source: Michael Yoshino

explained by the fact that there is a lower percentage of joint ventures among U.S. than among Japanese subsidiaries abroad. In joint ventures, the Japanese leave the top "ceremonial" posts to the local entrepreneur—a concession which is viewed cynically by some Indonesian and Thai observers.

When the Japanese give positions like personnel director to

Table 15

Americans in Management Positions in US Firms in Thailand and Indonesia.

In percentage of firms surveyed

	Thailand	Indonesia
A. Top management position, e.g. President, Chairman of the Board	68%	67%
B. Top operating management position	43	58
C. Top financial position	16	27
D. Top production position	21	43
E. Top sales/marketing position	23	33
F. Top personnel/industrial relations position	11	20
G. Top technical position	33	50
H. Top administrative position	8	22

Source: Business International Corporation, New York.

local employees they are met with the same cynical reaction. The result, says Panglaykim, "is that in the event of labor or tax problems, etc., the Indonesian representative is held responsible, while all decisions on pricing, raw materials, etc., continue to be decided by the Japanese partners." The Indonesian partner is, in fact, "a well-paid front," said S. B. Judono, head of the Institute for Economic and Social Research at the University of Indonesia.

Judono remarked in an interview that "the Indonesian partner is in fact dictated to in his dealings with the Japanese because he has no outside leverage. Everything—his credit, his transportation—is supplied or controlled by the Japanese." This, as we have seen, is the "package deal." As the Sumatran entrepreneur Ali Noorluddin said, it leaves the Indonesian partner "just a man holding a shed, with no technology being transferred from the Japanese to the Indonesians."

The riots during the Tanaka visit in 1974 have apparently not brought about any radical changes in Japanese attitudes in 1975. On December 20, 1973, just before the visit, Sydney Schanberg of the *New York Times* had reported from Jakarta:

> A man who had a 51 percent interest in a textile mill said the Japanese would not allow him in the front office. Another, a partner in a shrimp venture, said that he was not allowed on the boats and that no Indonesian crewman was admitted to the bridge.

> Still another Indonesian who had joined in a shrimp-freezing venture said his Japanese partner had shifted the company bank account and had transferred $100,000 to Tokyo without telling him and would not give him any idea what prices they were getting.

> Such complaints often crop up in a visitor's conversations with Indonesians. They say that the Japanese are ruthless and unscrupulous in business, that they block Indonesians from important jobs and that they pay Indonesians less than Japanese for identical work.

The package deal and its discriminatory implications also offend the Thai. "The plant is put up by Japanese technicians," Ob Vasuratana, president of the Thai Board of Trade, said in Bangkok, "all the raw materials come from Japan, the procurement manager is Japanese, and what he procures is expensive."

"Responsible positions are limited to Japanese," Ob added, "and they do not pass on the technology to the Thai." He further complained of Japanese reluctance to hire Thai staff. In a Japanese restaurant in Bangkok, all the waitresses were Japanese, and in the Japan Air Lines office, thirty of the staff were Japanese, compared to only three Americans in the Pan American office. The "confidential" explanation given by Japanese for this practice is the laziness of the indigenous worker.

A highly placed Japanese diplomat in Bangkok expressed the feeling in an interview that "the Thai are not prepared to absorb technology." He said the Japanese would be happy to employ local workers because "they are cheaper," but there are not many who are technically qualified. And Kazuko Tomita, a young labor expert on Thailand with the Tokyo Institute for Social Problems in Asia, while not absolving the Japanese (she, in fact, criticizes the presence of her countrymen in Thailand), recalled that Chinese employers also look down on their Thai workers saying, "Thais are so lazy, they just sit and they don't work; they are so stupid." She said she had told the Chinese employers off: "How could you ask them to be intelligent when you pay them so little?"

Franklin M. Proud, managing editor of the Bangkok magazine, *Business in Thailand*, stressed that one important reason the Japanese do not pass along the technology to the local workers is that, contrary to normal Japanese practice, they are not employed for life. "They [Thai employees] move from competitor to competitor," he observed, and there is nothing to stop them from sharing trade secrets. The distrust is aggravated by the fact that some local trainees returning from Japan are "lured away," as Yoshino reports in his Harvard Business School survey, "to more attractive positions with local firms or to more responsible positions with subsidiaries of other foreign companies." Thus, it would appear that the actual exclusion of Thai workers from the permanent vertical structure provides the Japanese with the excuse for not trusting them. Another expert observer, James C. Abegglen of the Boston Consulting Group, suggested in an interview that while exclusion or discrimination by Japanese may not be defensible, Thai or Indonesian workers may feel a kind of "complex resentment" against the Japanese for being "fellow Asians." The implication here is that Southeast Asians may, in fact, be less resentful of their former colonial masters because they continue somehow to feel inferior to them—a leftover of colonial education.

But the preponderance of evidence seems to support the feeling that the Japanese trust the local workers less and treat them less equally than do other foreign employers. Ob Vasuratana's example of Japan Air Lines is not an isolated case. The same thing is said in the Heller report (*The Economic and Social Impact of Foreign Investment in Hawaii*) about Japan Air Lines' policies in Hawaii.

Ironically, the former colonial masters seem to be displaying more trust in the local workers. The love-hate relationship between the Indonesians and the Dutch appears to have just about dropped the "hate" component. At Bandung, the site of the Asian-African Conference of 1955 which I attended as a Philippine delegate and where the postwar wave of anticolonialism and anti-Caucasianism reached a peak from which it has not descended significantly, the best-loved investors today appear to be the Dutch from Unilever and

Phillips. In 1973, the governor of Bandung was quoted singing the praises of the former masters of Indonesia and speaking forceful criticisms of the Japanese. He seems to reflect the general feeling among the people in his area, where obviously there is no hangover inferiority complex toward the Dutch: The Dutch and other Westerners seem to trust the Indonesians and appear to treat them as equals. But the Japanese do not.

Tokyo *Newsweek* Bureau Chief Bernard Krisher told me about his own experience at the Chase Manhattan Bank branch in Jakarta:

> I walked in to talk to the [American] manager there and he insisted on calling his Indonesian number two. The Indonesian did not want to come in. I also said, "I don't want to talk to him. I want to talk to you—about your image of the Japanese. I've talked to enough Indonesians. I want to get a third country view, so we don't need him." I said that in front of the Indonesian because I've been there so often and I talk to them as an equal, too. I said, "I don't need your opinion. Let me talk to this guy from New York."
>
> The whole thing was a lot of equal give-and-take. Here was a manager who did not want to talk without his Indonesian assistant. The Japanese would be quite different. He would simply shut the door.

Yoshino has a rational explanation for this behavior of Japanese managers which is related to the structure of the vertical *ie.* "The Japanese manager who must head the foreign subsidiary," he explains in his Harvard study, "is so wedded to the traditional managerial system of his country that he would find it impossible to manage an organization without the support of subordinates who share the same work style." There is also "a strong need for the subsidiary to interact with the parent company in the solicitation of support and resources, [and here] the communications role is particularly important." This brings us back to the problem of language and word interpretation. Yet even Japanese nationals (with obviously no language problem) who are recruited locally by the subsidiary find difficulty in being accepted as "full-fledged members of the organization" and become "mere functionaries and interpreters, regardless of seniority or experience."

Because of so much publicly discussed criticism of Japanese treatment of local workers, the more qualified among them are attracted to European or American firms. The marked preference for European or American employment is reflected in available formal surveys. In the 1974 Bangkok universities' survey of student opinion cited earlier, the question was asked, "When you have finished your studies, will you become a civil servant or work in a factory or a foreign company?" American, Australian, or European firms were preferred by 45.4 percent, the civil service by 25 percent, and a

Japanese firm by 10.8 percent. These percentages become dramatic when placed beside the figures of the Board of Investments on foreign investment in Thailand which show that, of registered foreign capital in 1960-74, the Japanese are credited with 41.8 percent; the United States, 14.41 percent; the United Kingdom and Western Europe, 9.71 percent; and Australia, 0.44 percent.

What emerge here are several vicious circles. The Japanese do not pass on their technology to the local workers because they are not on lifetime employment. But they are not on lifetime employment because they are not Japanese. The Japanese do not give local employees responsible positions because they are not qualified. They are not qualified because those who are qualified prefer to work for other foreign companies. They prefer other foreign companies because the Japanese do not give local workers responsible positions. The Japanese are clannish because of the communication problem. But they have a communication problem because of their clannish vertical system.

The biggest circle of all, the *cercle de résistance*, as it were, would require a century of evolution or one, perhaps bloody, moment of convulsion to break. Japan's vertical society produces her relentless dynamism. It also produces problems for her that defy solution. The only solution seems to be the overhauling of her society. But the overhauling of her society would spoil her dynamism. It is a vicious dilemma which the Japanese are at the moment understandably not eager to solve.

The Japanese Compulsion to Corrupt and the Local Readiness to be Corrupted

"Since Japan's advance into the Korean Peninsula," says Kyoto University political scientist Toru Yano (described by some Japanese intellectuals as "hawkish"), "Japanese diplomacy has pursued the policy of digging up 'pro-Japanese' groups and placing them in power, in order that Japan might gain freedom of action."

In the light of history book accounts of the methods of nineteenth century British imperialism and the current U.S. congressional revelations on the activities of American agencies and companies abroad, there would seem to be nothing terribly original or exciting about this particular feature of Japanese policy. The tactic of influencing foreign officials is as old as the Biblical kingdoms.

But something in the "bicycle action" of the Japanese economy creates a unique dimension in the crisis potential of the Japanese presence in Southeast Asia. The system puts a performance pressure upon them and the hardest-driving contributor to this pressure appears to be the credit component in the investment pattern.

As has been seen, the investment brinkmanship or edge-of-bankruptcy policy of Japanese financing permits domestic and overseas companies to capitalize themselves with a shockingly high percentage of borrowings, sometimes 80 percent or more. In the overseas joint venture plan, the money that is loaned to the capital-short local partner is not given to him directly. It is channeled through the intermediary Japanese firms which have provided the guarantee. Thus, the primary responsibility for making good on the loan remains on the shoulders of the Japanese.

The loan is usually medium or short term. While the Bank of Japan is always standing by to rescue companies holding loans whose terms are perilously close to termination, no normal Japanese would risk losing face with overdue loans. Here, then, is the performance pressure. Japanese businessmen must perform or else. Harvard Professor Yoshino admits that there are "certain peculiarities of the Japanese situation—notably a heavy reliance on debt with high fixed charges" which adds "further pressure for capacity utilization." The dangers attendant upon the system are admitted even by Japanese organizations like the Nomura Research Institute, which in 1973 warned of "friction resulting from the attempts at securing early return on short-term investments."[11] "Friction" is a euphemism for what a distinguished Indonesian intellectual characterized as the compulsion to corrupt. "They have to show profits right away," he said in Jakarta, "therefore they rush to indulge in bribery." He said that a European ambassador had told him, "Until recently I advised my countrymen not to give bribes. But I have stopped because the Japanese squeeze them out!"

Jacob Utomo, editor of the Catholic paper, *Kompas*, which survived the press shutdowns that followed the anti-Tanaka riots and which now claims the largest circulation in Indonesia, told me he thought that "the Japanese motivation for profit is too rough." He said that as a consequence the Japanese "misused Indonesian government officials."

Charges of Japanese "misuse" of Indonesian officials were of such volume that, as D. H. Assegaff, chief editor of the progovernment paper, *Suara Karya*, recalled in Jakarta, students had organized the *Komite Anti Korupsi* long before the Tanaka visit and had demonstrated in front of Parliament and the president's residence. The newspaper *Indonesia Raya*, which was suppressed after the riots, had charged that an army general, a high official in the government oil monopoly, "gave low prices to Japan in return for alleged payoffs." Other papers had also "exposed the Japanese business involvements of two key Suharto aides" who were top generals. The report further said the "Obi and Taliabu timber companies gave well-publicized directorships to leading military men in return for alleged special favors." The foreign minister, Adam

---

[11]Nomura Research Institute, *Multinationalization of Japanese Companies* (Tokyo: Nomura Research Report, June 25, 1973), p. 12.

Malik, decried the "tremendous temptations" offered by the Japanese "before our local administrators."

President Suharto himself apparently took cognizance of the charges. In 1970, he formed the Commission of Four to investigate corruption. It made some findings criticizing "loosely defined concessions" made by state timber enterprises to Japanese interests. University of Indonesia economist S. B. Judono referred to an interview to government measures to curb the overtones of corruption by declaring nightclubs off limits to government officials, banning gifts to them, and limiting their official receptions to 2,000 guests. All this has not seemed to quash private talk against the lavish living of officials and generals. The army itself appears to be divided on the question. An authoritative source reports that among Indonesian army officers there are those, "especially among the younger, academy-trained generation, who have become deeply disturbed by the widespread business activities of the older generation which have brought the army into much public disrepute."[12]

To be sure, there are Japanese businessmen who throw back these charges. A March 2, 1973, *Washington Post* article reported that Shizuo Kawanami, director of Balikpapan Forest Industries in Kalimantan, blames all Southeast Asian countries "whose local officials use Japanese as scapegoats for their own failures" and warns that there is not much hope for distribution of wealth "unless this corruption stops." Yet, the evidence pointing to Japanese involvement in corruption appears to be found everywhere. In Bangkok, the respected rector of Thammasat University, Dr. Puey Ungphakorn, who is cautious in his remarks on corruption, admitted to me that there were reports of Japanese support for a well-known Thai general who was linked with a Japanese firm during the dictatorship that ended in October, 1973.

The noted Thai intellectual, Kien Theeravit, is more detailed in his bill of particulars. In *The Japanese-Thai Economic Interaction*, he mentions a survey through which "it was discovered that a number of Thai officials have been underhandedly earning money from Japanese companies." He charges that Japanese ventures "attempt to maximize their profits at the expense of legality," that Japanese shipping companies and tourist agencies "practice tax evasion and bribery," that Japanese restaurants and entertainment businesses "pay few legal fees to the government but much tea money to local officials," and that Japanese visitors "usually renew their visas . . . by sending 'gifts' to immigration officers." In the "Look at Japan" exhibition at Chulalongkorn University, posters asked the question: "Are high-ranking Thai officials, who are corrupt and hold

---

[12]Harold Crouch, "The '15th January Affair' in Indonesia," *Dyason House Papers* (Melbourne: Australian Institute of International Affairs, August 1974), p.2.

shares in the investors' enterprises the loophole for the Japanese to take advantage of this country?" "Thai students," says Kanagawa Governor Kazuji Nagasu, "have found the proper channel for nationalism in the overthrow of the Thanom regime, which was so intimately and so corruptly linked to Japan." Nagasu also charges "private collusion and corruption [between] Japan's conservative politicians and businessmen and the political leaders" in countries receiving Japanese "aid."[13]

Thus, Japanese and non-Japanese alike are disturbed by the Japanese compulsion to corrupt. "The Japanese want to save time," Newsweek's irrepressible Bernard Krisher said in a Tokyo interview. "They are very eager to corrupt, unlike Americans and Westerners who wait to be asked." In outlying Indonesian cities, they get telephone equipment or even drivers' licenses in one day "because these government officials are already attuned to the Japanese eagerness to pay."

The main office in Tokyo sanctions this "eagerness to pay" in its accounting procedures. Receipts for these under-the-table transactions, says Krisher, are accepted as evidence of business expense. Corruption is thus institutionalized. It has to be, for the "bicycle action" requires it lest the wheels slow down to a wobbly speed and the giant economy topple over.

In mid-1975, U.S. congressional investigations confirmed that large-scale corruption of host country officials is not the monopoly of Japanese companies. U.S. multinationals were discovered to have expended millions in Europe, Latin America, Japan and the Middle East to influence local officials in the race for government contracts. Perhaps spurred by the investigations into taking its own initiative, the U.S.-based Merck & Company, one of the world's largest drug firms (1974 total sales: $1.3 billion), announced in September, 1975, that an "internal investigation" had thus far revealed that "a few Merck people" had made questionable payments of $140,000 to employees of governments in Africa and the Middle East and that "immediate steps were taken to prevent any such payments in the future." Even if overseas corruption has in fact been as institutionalized among U.S. companies as it appears to be among the Japanese, there are signs of U.S. efforts, government and private, to "deinstitutionalize" it. Japanese reaction to the revelations of Lockheed bribery in their country was hysterical yet there are so far no visible moves in Japan to investigate bribery by Japanese abroad. Until such moves are made and publicized, we may not obtain access to solid figures on the dimensions of the Japanese corruptive thrust into Southeast Asia. It could be, in fact, no worse than the corruptive efforts of other foreign investors. But for the moment, local

---

[13]Nagasu, "Super-Illusions of an Economic Superpower," p. 162.

perception would seem to regard it as the most massive. It should be remembered, of course, that Japanese foreign investment in the region is also the largest.

Meanwhile, institutionalized corruption has already caused two major collisions for the Tokyo Express. According to the *New York Times* (January 16, 1974), the Indonesian students who built bonfires with Japanese-made cars, trucks, and motorcycles in January, 1974, were "angry over widespread Japanese payoffs to high Government officials" and wanted visiting Prime Minister Tanaka to know it. The same sentiments were shouted by Thai students when they cornered Tanaka at the Erawan Hotel in Bangkok.

Is compulsion to corruption after all part of the ritualism of the dynamic, vertical *ie*? Is it stretching it too far to relate the ease with which Japanese give gifts to foreign officials to the periodic holiday offering to superiors with which inferiors in the company *ie* must routinely but heartily comply as part of the "escalator process" of the permanent employment and seniority system?

Nakane reminds us that "Japan was able to attain such a pitch of industrialization so swiftly . . . because the wheels of the vehicle had been made long before modernization, and it required only changes in the type of passenger carried and the direction taken." Changing the "structural configuration" would have meant disorder which "would have lowered the speed of the process and would have brought far greater suffering."[14]

The current Japanese experience abroad could be an indication that the passenger, in fact, has not changed and will not change unless the vehicle is altered. But that cannot or should not happen for, as Nakane says, there would be "far greater suffering."

Add another vicious circle.

---

[14]Nakane, *Japanese Society*, p. 119.

VI

The Chinese Connection

"China will never be a collaborator of Japan; she will always be a competitor," *Business in Thailand*'s managing editor Franklin Proud told me in Bangkok.

Proud may have been projecting a long-range view. In the short run, China's new pragmatic policy appears to permit it to engage in fairly meaningful economic collaboration with Japan, allowing its current ambitions for labor-intensive industrial development to mesh with Japan's avid search for cheap labor overseas. Rand Corporation sources report that 30,000 of the total annual Japanese truck production of 100,000 trucks are being made in Chinese communes. In addition, Japanese firms have farmed out in China the manufacture of such auxiliary items as jacks, monkey wrenches, and tool kits.[1]

Given the sharp ideological cleavage between the two countries, this postwar Japanese economic beachhead on Chinese soil must be rated as a significant achievement. As blood is thicker than water, culture would here appear to be thicker than ideology. And where the ideological cleavage does not exist, as with the twenty-one million overseas Chinese, cultural affinity seems to have produced even closer and, to some, more disturbing collaboration (some would call it conspiracy) between Japanese and Chinese, though, as will be seen, conflicting capitalist interests could also breed an explosive rivalry between them.

In the vertical vision of the Japanese, the Chinese are one of the boys. "We seem," observed cultural anthropologist Masao Kunihiro, "to reserve a very warm spot somewhere in our hearts for things

---

[1] Richard J. Barnet and Ronald E. Müller, *Global Reach* (New York: Simon and Schuster, 1974), p.171.

Chinese under whatever form of regime or ideology." Kunihiro thinks that the sense of war guilt is, for this reason, not as pronounced toward Southeast Asian Countries as it is toward China.

The observation of Mohammad Sadli, the minister of mines and a leading Indonesian technocrat, that Japanese do not look down on Chinese and that they are "natural allies" is openly supported by Japanese businessmen like Yasuhiro Sannomiya in Bangkok, who says that the Japanese and Chinese enjoy "a natural division of labor" in Thailand, where the Chinese control the distribution of Japanese manufactured goods and go into manufacturing only by tolerance of or in joint venture with the Japanese. In the rural areas, Chinese control the crop credit (as has been the case in Indonesia and the Philippines) and then control the export of produce to Japan.

The Japanese preference for Chinese partners is resented by the Thais. Dr. Kien Theeravit, noted Thai political scientist, says that the Thai people look at the Japanese as Asians and do not forgive them for not acting in accordance with what is expected. But Teichiro Morinaga, head of the Tokyo Stock Exchange, explained why the Japanese are inexorably attracted to the overseas Chinese: "They are the most hard-working people in the area in addition to their local knowledge, their business experience, and the useful horizontal ties they have across the borders." The distinguished retired ambassador, Nobuhiko Ushiba, confirmed this to me in Tokyo. He said the overseas Chinese were preferred "not for reasons of cultural affinity but for the reasons that they have more money and they have more business experience." Yet, according to the Heller Report, in Hawaii, where education is universal and Americans of Chinese ancestry enjoy no marked advantage over other ethnic groups in business training, Japanese firms tend to hire per capita more Chinese than any other non-Japanese group (except for Koreans who tend to look like Japanese), thus apparently confirming the "cultural affinity" theory.

The Japanese embassy in Jakarta has confirmed that more than 70 percent of Japanese investors in Indonesia have taken on ethnic Chinese as their joint-venture partners. This is particularly interesting in a country where thousands of Chinese were killed in the bloodbath of 1965 and where attempts at assimilation (including forced adoption of Indonesian names) have not been a spectacular success. The changing of names, in fact, appears to have camouflaged the continued Chinese control of the economy. "They are really capitalizing on the name changing," observed Indonesian businessman Ali Noorluddin.

"Do not underestimate the overseas Chinese," Noorluddin warned. "They are strong and they help each other; they have more experience and more exposure to trade practices, while among Indonesians very few come from a business background.

"But I am an exception," Noorluddin quickly added. "I am a Sumatran. We Sumatrans have always been in business as a tradition, and the Japanese have started to believe in us. . . . There are some good Javanese businessmen also," he added, with a wink.

But the Javanese, who, in Noorluddin's words, "are more government, academic, and culture oriented, unlike the Sumatrans who travel and move around," tend to view the Chinese question with more than a wink. The government officially recognizes the distinction between "indigenous" (i.e., Indonesian) and "nonindigenous" (i.e., Chinese) businessmen and has taken steps to protect the former against the latter or, at least, to improve the former's position vis-à-vis the latter.

PT BAHANA is a state-owned company which screens budding indigenous entrepreneurs for recommendation to financing institutions which may grant them as much as 75 percent investment credit to their original 25 percent investment at the low rate of 1 percent interest a month. The program is designed to organize the indigenous entrepreneur and give him a fighting chance against the nonindigenous businessman. "Three hundred and sixty years of Dutch colonization," said the company's president, Susilo Sadardi, in Jakarta, "did not enable the Indonesians to build up their own capacity, for in those days the nonindigenous entrepreneurs were used by the Dutch as a buffer between the indigenous and the colonizers."

The next step would be to bring small indigenous investors together so that they might present stronger possibilities for partnership with the Japanese. The State Development Bank (BABINDO) currently attempts to provide financing on a limited scale for prospective joint-venture partners; but, as we have seen, Japanese loan rates are so competitive that even nonindigenous partners (i.e., the Chinese) are forced to accept the "package deal."

Some Indonesians do not regard the conflict between the indigenous and the nonindigenous with too much alarm. Thee Kianwie, assistant director of the University of Indonesia's Institute of Economic and Social Research, finds "nothing sinister" in the Japanese-Chinese partnership since, "as in other Asian countries, the distributive trade is in the hands of the Chinese." Yet, Franklin B. Weinstein, in his remarkable study of the Indonesian elite's view of the world, found that, "as for the Chinese and Japanese, it was perfectly clear that they are regarded as dangerous, aggressive alien forces; not infrequently they were grouped together by the Indonesian leaders as the 'yellow peril.' " Weinstein noted that to many Indonesians, "as an economic threat, China, Hong Kong, Singapore, and the Indonesian Chinese were indistinguishable from one another." He also mentioned a prediction by an Indonesian technocrat that "only if economic development were to fail badly would the subversive threat of China again become the principal danger; if development were to succeed to any reasonable degree, Japan would be the greater threat."[2]

Herbert Feith, the noted Australian political scientist and Indonesia-watcher, is not impressed with Indonesian efforts to build up indigenous entrepreneurship. "It has suited the generals to allow the Chinese to build up their organization while they [the generals] have done little to encourage an ethos of building, achieving, or producing among highly placed ethnic Indonesians," he observed in a 1973 paper presented at a Monash University seminar on the Indonesian economy. "The Chinese business community is not better off than before," he added, since they remain "amenable to being squeezed." The Chinese businessmen are "protected" in their joint ventures with the Japanese.

Soedjatmoko, the distinguished Indonesian intellectual and consultant to the Indonesian Planning Board (BAPENAS), warns of the "hidden political cost" for the future in the Japanese rush, "due to lack of time," to nonindigenous or Chinese partners in order to make quick profits. He suggests that a Japanese shift to long-term lending and long-range profit-taking might encourage the Japanese investors to take on less-prepared and lesser-financed indigenous partners and head off what appears to be an eventual political explosion. In a 1973 speech delivered at Sophia University, Sadli voiced the cautious government approach: "The government's policy is to fully utilize the capabilities of the Chinese, but now the trick is how to do it without disturbing delicate social and racial balances. It is a difficult thing and we will always be unsuccessful, we will always be dissatisfied."

"It is academic," a friend told me in Bangkok, "to look for figures on what percentage of Japanese joint ventures in Thailand are with Chinese. Theoretically, there are no Chinese left in Thailand. They have all become Thai." Actually, about half of the three million Chinese in Thailand are of Thai citizenship, and many of the noncitizens are married to Thais. On the surface, the assimilation program in Thailand has been more successful than its counterpart in Indonesia. Religion may have something to do with it. "Unlike in Malaysia," writes the Japanese intellectual, Kobayashi Keiji, "there is no religious strife between the Chinese and the local people in Thailand, hence the relationship between the two ethnic groups is the smoothest of any in Southeast Asia."[3] Deja Boonchuchuy of the Thai Board of Investments was careful to note, however, that the two ethnic groups were still "socially different," although the People's Republic of China itself had observed that Chinese assimila-

---

[2]Franklin B. Weinstein, "The Uses of Foreign Policy in Indonesia" (Cornell University unpublished doctoral thesis, 1972).

[3]Kobayashi Keiji, "An Asian Image of Japan," *Japan Interpreter* 7 (Spring 1971): 134-35.

tion in Thailand was the "fastest." He noted that the Chinese in Thailand are Mahayana Buddhists while the Thais belong to the Hinayana Buddhist tradition. He then volunteered the information that the "big banking people" are of Chinese descent.

Indeed, the cracks in the surface assimilation are more than religious. As we have seen earlier, Japanese and Thais alike recognize the continuing de facto separate identity of the Chinese in Thailand, and the Japanese avidly seek them out as partners and distributors. Japan Trade Center's President Yasuyuki Matsuo said he believes that "no one in Thailand but the Chinese have business ability." Ob Vasuratana admitted that the Chinese in Thailand were "totally assimilated" but added in the same breath that the "Chinese are better prepared for business." Franklin Proud confirmed that the Chinese community in Thailand was the most integrated in Asia but also added that K. Y. Chow (also known as Chao Chaokhuanyuen), the millionaire industrialist behind the giant petrochemical and Kra canal projects from which the Japanese have withdrawn, was "often criticized because he came from China."

Dr. Puey Ungphakorn, the noted Thai educator, observed in Bangkok that, besides the question of ideology, one of the obstacles to normalizing relations between Peking and the Thai government was the existence of a strong Chinese minority in Thailand. He also foresaw the emergence of a rivalry between China and Japan in spite of the flourishing partnerships between Japanese and overseas Chinese businessmen. This rivalry was discounted as a short-term possibility by Saburo Ohkita, Japan's leading economic planner, who believes China will practice "an inward-looking policy in the next few years [and] may have ideological but not economic influence" on Southeast Asia. He is confident that Japan's economic influence would "be much longer."

But talk of an emerging rivalry between the strongly capitalist overseas Chinese and the Japanese appears less speculative and brings into focus one of the more fascinating questions that divide many in Japan and Southeast Asia, namely, what role did the overseas Chinese play in the anti-Tanaka riots in Jakarta and Bangkok?

When Japan overtook West Germany in 1969 to become the world's third-richest economy, China suddenly realized that it had at its doorstep, instead of a revisionist fellow communist or a distantly based capitalist-imperialist, a very successful Asian capitalist dominating Southeast Asia, which China had regarded as its future sphere of influence. China's first response to this new reality was a propaganda campaign, launched by Chou En-lai during a visit to Pyongyang in 1971. Every day, Radio Peking, the New China News Agency, and all the Chinese propaganda outlets turned out charges against the new Japanese expansionism and militarism. In 1971, Chou En-lai was repeatedly quoted on Japan's determination to reoccupy South Korea and Taiwan.

"This was the only way," recalled Derek Davies in an interview, "that China could react since she did not have an economic response to Japan's economic muscle." The campaign had an effect on the overseas Chinese and on the indigenous Southeast Asians, the "radical students and those against foreign capital," reviving memories of the Pacific war and the old fears of the "Co-Prosperity Sphere." "I would link the riots in Southeast Asia with that campaign," Davies asserted, pointing out that after the disturbances it seemed to have suited China to "switch off and start the process of reconciliation." Indeed, it was not long after the riots that Chou En-lai gave Japan the fatherly counsel that it would do very well to get even closer to the United States.

Davies's theory is supported by Japanese of varying backgrounds. T. Aoki, a Japanese anthropologist who had studied at Chulalongkorn University and spent two years as a Buddhist monk in Bangkok, recalled that just before the boycott of Japanese goods in 1972 and also before the anti-Tanaka demonstration in January, 1974, there seemed to be evidence that "the anti-Japanese movement was a conspiracy of Chinese merchants," not for ideological but for purely "commercial" reasons. Presumably he would distinguish these Chinese merchants from the Chinese partners of the Japanese joint ventures. Kazuko Tomita of the Tokyo Institute for Social Problems in Asia felt the anti-Japanese feeling in Thailand was "exerted by some financially influential people like the Chinese." It is not lost on ranking Japanese diplomats in Bangkok that among the students who assaulted the Daimaru department store were sons of rich Chinese. They believe the local Chinese were basically against Japanese economic influence and "may have inspired" anti-Japanese action.

In Indonesia, Susilo Sadardi of PT BAHANA pointed out that the Japanese and not the Americans or Europeans, who concentrate on extractive operations like oil drilling or mining, are the competitors of the Chinese. He said he felt "the Chinese are using the indigenous Indonesians to voice their sentiments [and that] the indigenous Indonesians do not see through the half-truths, since Japanese investments hit the Chinese rather than the indigenous." Yusuf Panglaykim, technocrat in the Centre for Strategic and International Studies in Jakarta, whose name indicates he may be of Chinese descent, thought, "China may have told the Japanese to withdraw from the Hong Kong subway project."

Ob Vasuratana implied that the Thai Chinese favored the anti-Japanese demonstrations. He said, "The businessmen were quite happy with the results of the demonstrations." Most Thai businessmen are Chinese.

Against this amorphous body of opinion is arrayed a varied group, including some Japanese. Dr. Frances Starner, a keen student of Southeast Asia and formerly with the *Far Eastern Economic Review*, takes issue with her former editor. She says that the Japanese

have shown themselves so inflexible even in seminars and confer-
ences that there is no need for the Chinese "to get things going."
"Besides," she adds, "you have the other evidence that there were
people of Chinese ancestry [in Indonesia called *Chukongs*] who had
worked quite joyfully with the Japanese where there was money to
be made in doing so." Some of those Chinese had, indeed, been
hounded out by the demonstrators.

Indonesian economist S. B. Judono thought overseas Chinese
support of the demonstrations "impossible" because of the close
"natural" collaboration between overseas Chinese and Japanese.
Two ranking Japanese diplomats in Jakarta recalled that while there
was some suspicion of local Chinese communist instigation of the
anti-Tanaka riots, the evidence showed that "the Chinese suffered
the biggest damage" with their restaurants, shops, etc., set on fire.
There was a touch of irony in the fact that the Japanese sustained no
real damage in the burning of Japanese-made cars, trucks, and
motorcycles, since these were owned mostly by indigenous or
Chinese Indonesians. The diplomats said their embassy had mis-
calculated the anti-Chinese sentiment in Indonesia and that "in a
few years it will be difficult to distinguish between Japanese and
Chinese" in popular demonstrations.

On August 5, 1973, a large anti-Chinese riot occurred in Bandung during which, from 4:00 p.m. to 1:00 a.m., the poor and unem-
ployed of Bandung expressed their resentment against the wealthy
Chinese business community by damaging more than 1,500 shops
and houses. Much the same thing took place during the anti-Tanaka
riots according to an on-the-spot *New York Times* report. The report
stressed that the demonstrators sacked and set fire to "stores and
businesses that sold Japanese products, especially those owned by
overseas Chinese, [that the] ugliest scene occurred at the Pasar
Senen shopping center, where thousands of rioters looted the Chi-
nese-owned stores and stalls and started fires, [and that] the students resent the special privileges held by the Chinese residents." It
is also significant that the immediate remedial measures adopted by
the Indonesian government after the riots were not directed at the
Japanese but at the local Chinese. The government announced, on
January 23, "a series of tough new measures designed to curtail assets of resident Chinese businessmen and eliminate corruption in
government."

The Japanese diplomats' prediction that in a few years demonstrators will not distinguish between Japanese and Chinese may sum
up the extent of the crisis potential in the Chinese connection of
Japanese economic activity in Southeast Asia. A distinguished
Indonesian journalist put it this way in Jakarta: "When it explodes
again, the people will turn against the Chinese as well as the
Japanese—and even the Americans."

VII

"Anti-Revolutionary A Priori"

If an explosion comes, as predicted, why would people turn against the Chinese, Japanese, *and* Americans? Has not the evidence, in fact, shown that, in comparison with the behavior of the so-called ugly Japanese, that of the Americans—and Europeans— has apparently acquired for them a new, perhaps more attractive face?

"All Southeast Asian societies," says Kyoto University political scientist Toru Yano, "have a dual structure, characterized by a sharp contrast between the rich and the poor. In advancing into the region, Japan concerns herself only with the upper stratum of the dual structure. For this reason, Japan's advance is antirevolutionary a priori and in favor of maintaining the status quo."[1]

The Western advance shares this basic characteristic with that of Japan. True, Western aid has had its flashes of reformism which in some conservative societies have seemed, in fact, revolutionary, such as U.S. support for democratic land reform. But the fundamental assumption of Western investment resembles that of the Japanese, i.e., it is doing the developing countries a favor because these countries need capital and technology, and the only way they can get it in sufficient volume is through direct foreign investment.

Some Americans have questioned this assumption, even in the context of U.S. history. U.S. consumer advocate Ralph Nader, testifying in 1974 before the United Nations Group of Eminent Persons to

---

[1] Toru Yano, "Postwar Structure of 'Nanshin,'" *Japan Echo* 1 (1974): 41.

Study the Impact of Multinational Corporations on Development and on International Relations, said he believes the United States "would not have developed as rapidly as it did, if it had not been for the fact that we took credits instead of equity in developing industry." He recalled that in the nineteenth century "a great deal of money was borrowed from England, and it came in the form of credit and not so much in the form of equity ownership." To American investors who deplore today's nationalistic trends which discourage foreign investments in developing nations, Nader has this reminder: "We had a very chauvinistic approach to foreign multinational corporations in the nineteenth century. We should remember that the United States in the nineteenth century and the early twentieth century was about as antagonistic to foreign ownership as any nation in the market world today. In fact, it was almost a *casus belli* for a foreign corporation to come in and take over a large land area or a segment of the industry."

"Japan's phenomenal postwar development, it must be remembered," says political scientist Richard Barnet, "was based largely on the exclusion of foreign investment,"[2] though not, it should be noted, without substantial foreign aid. Michael Yoshino recalled that during the 1950s and much of the 1960s, Japan imposed almost ironclad restrictions on import and investment. William Lockwood writes that, aside from electric utilities, "foreign investment in business enterprise in [prewar] Japan was rather insignificant in amount." It was $70 million in 1913 and $100 million in 1929. In addition, in 1929, Y579 million of Japanese corporate securities, mostly electric power companies' bonds, were held abroad. All this, however, was only one-twentieth of the Y16.4 billion (about $8 billion) which represented the total paid-up capital and reserves of Japanese industry.

As for technology, Lockwood recalls that Japan hired "hundreds of experts" from abroad and sent out Japanese by the score to acquire expertise from Europe and the United States. The first of these was apparently "a Japanese artist, first employed by the Mitsuis to paint a portrait of [Commodore] Perry [and] later dispatched to study ships and machinery abroad."[3] This, in probably much less regimented fashion, was how the United States acquired technology from England and Europe.

Alexander Wroniak, writing on the technology gap between the Western world and Japan on the one hand and the communist countries on the other, observes that, since 1949, Soviet experts and managers have averaged 2,200 visits abroad yearly. By contrast,

---

[2]Barnet and Müller, *Global Reach*, p. 156.

[3]William Lockwood, *The Economic Development of Japan* (Princeton, New Jersey: Princeton University Press, 1968), pp. 49-50 and 321.

"the number of Japanese visitors in 1963 exceeded 18,000." Wroniak feels the communist policy of discouraging foreign travel "indirectly retards the introduction of new methods, processes, and procedures."[4] The Japanese, on the other hand, with greater language barriers, are determined to have their technicians travel abroad to pick up the latest technology.

Having learned by traveling, the Japanese then set up their "ironclad restrictions on investment" which, Yoshino points out, placed them "in an excellent bargaining position to obtain foreign technologies. . . . Between 1950 and 1972, Japanese firms entered into 17,600 licensing agreements for which they paid $3.3 billion in royalties. . . . The technology thus obtained," he adds, "covered practically every field of modern industry."[5]

We have seen how Southeast Asian countries accuse Japanese companies of reluctance in transferring technology. The implication is that the Japanese are selfish. The stock Japanese excuse is that few Southeast Asians are prepared for the transfer. Toru Yano said bluntly in Kyoto that "Southeast Asia cannot absorb Japan's technology because it is so sophisticated." This is a statement that should be scrutinized. Thousands of Filipino doctors, engineers, nurses, accountants are scattered all over the world—in the United States, Canada, Australia, and the Middle East—for lack of skilled jobs at home. Indonesian embassy sources in Washington state that as of 1972 there were twenty-five state-supported engineering schools in Indonesia with a total enrollment of 13,778 and thirty-one private engineering schools with a total enrollment of 7,463. There were also 4,846 enrolled in government and private academies studying for a Bachelor of Science degree.

However, there is nothing so "sophisticated" about Japanese capital that Southeast Asia, with its inexpensive labor, cannot absorb it. Yet, is this capital being transferred to Japan's southern neighbors?

The answer, apparently, is that it is not—at least not much of it. The 1970 findings by Fernando Falnzylber in his United Nations study on the strategy of global corporations in Latin America are that the corporations tend to use savings of the host country for their local operations rather than to bring in capital from the developed nations. This is probably true in the Southeast Asian context too.[6]

Thai Board of Trade President Ob Vasuratana, not known for basically antiforeign investment views, told me in Bangkok that "when the Board of Investments approves a joint venture it is under-

---

[4]Alexander Wroniak, "Technological Transfer in Eastern Europe: Receiving Countries," East-West Trade and the Technology Gap, ed. Stanislaw Wasowski (New York: Praeger, 1970), p. 110.

[5]Yoshino, "The Multinational Spread of Japanese Enterprises."

[6]Barnet and Müller, Global Reach, p. 152.

stood that they bring in the money from Japan or elsewhere, *but most of them do not."* Foreign banks, including two Japanese, supply the credit. "The Tokyo and Mitsui banks use local depositors' money to enable Japanese to join with Thai partners," Vasuratana complains. Another expert confirms that Japanese "draw money from Thai banks for investment; that means they invest Thai money."

Figures on just how much of the loan and equity capital of joint ventures is taken from banks in Thailand, Indonesia, and other Southeast Asian countries have not been available. Falnzylber's finding that American multinationals finance their Latin American operations by as much as 83 percent from local funds might be questioned as an irrelevant factor for Southeast Asia. But other more relevant indicators in the Southeast Asian area are available.

A March, 1975, *Fortune* article on the First National City Bank of New York contains some relevant, and startling, facts. "Citibank," proclaims the article's headline, "makes more than three-fifths of its profits abroad." This figure represents profits made on the operations of its overseas branches and "excludes the profits made on foreign loans made in New York. . . . Perhaps the most startling fact of all," admits the business-oriented publication, "is that Citibank makes 40 percent of its profits in the underdeveloped world. That number is not generally known outside the bank, or even inside, and Citibank's rivals are both envious and incredulous when they hear it." Of the bank's global earnings, 15 percent comes from the Asia-Pacific region, which includes Indonesia, Thailand, and the Philippines; 9 percent from South America, and about 8 percent from South Asia, the Mideast, and Africa. The figures are startling—but what, after all, is wrong with making profits in underdeveloped countries in exchange for injecting massive capital into them for their development?

What massive capital? "Citibank's overseas branches," says *Fortune, "raise most of their money in their local markets"!* (Italics added.) And "Citibank's average cost of money in the poorer nations is further reduced by the bountiful supply of demand deposits it attracts" on which the bank pays interest whose "rates are nominal, ranging from about 1 to 3 percent." This money is then loaned "in local currencies to local businesses and individuals. Between $3 billion and $4 billion is lent in the poorer countries." The term "local businesses and individuals" is, of course, misleading. As has been seen, about the only ones in developing nations with the borrowing capacity for loans in the millions are the foreign multinationals and their joint ventures. Small indigenous enterprises with modest collateral simply cannot compete with the global corporations with their blue chip assets in bidding for commercial loans. This tends to confirm the complaint of the Thai business and academic leaders that Japanese and foreign investors do not actually bring in most of their venture capital. And it happens in Indonesia, too. More so, it

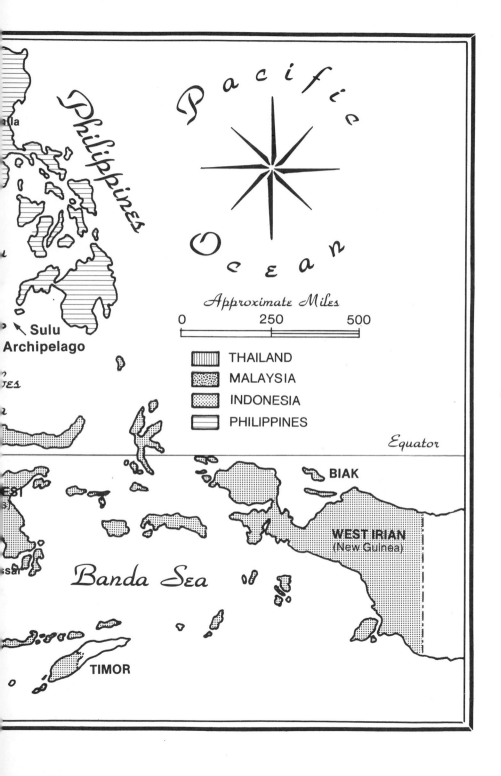

would seem, for as *Fortune* adds, "The profit margins on this end of the business are spectacular. They are so high, in fact, that Wriston [Citibank's chairman] is fond of saying: 'Around here it's Jakarta that pays the check.' "

But is not all this, after all, a "mobilization of capital," even of local capital, for local development, employment, and building up of foreign exchange reserves? We shall shortly look into the development and employment effect of these operations. As for foreign exchange reserves, *Fortune* reveals that when a U.S. multinational has profits in Indonesian *rupiahs* and wants to repatriate them, "Citibank can arrange transactions at a substantial profit" of at least $2,500 for each $1 million handled.

The repatriation operations in the Philippines, where the Marcos regime has instituted generous policies on foreign investments, have "maximized" profits. The *Fortune* account of these operations is worth reproducing in full:

> In some exchange markets, the bank maximizes its fees by running what is called a matched book. In the Philippines, for example, Citibank, which dominates the local market, will buy only as many pesos (for example, *from multinationals with local currency earnings*) as it can readily sell (for example, to exporters who have dollars to convert). By controlling its volume, the bank regulates the size of the fees. As a result, its foreign exchange earnings in the Philippines are enormous. *Last year, they accounted for about 5 percent of the bank's $89-million total foreign-exchange income.* (Italics added.)

The article indicates that "under stable conditions in a more competitive market" the most a bank can hope to earn in foreign exchange transactions is "five basis points" or "$500 for each $1 million handled." Assuming the Philippine market to be stable, Citibank in 1974 would have had to handle the export of $8.9 billion from the Philippines to earn 5 percent of $89 million or $4.45 million. Conversely, assuming that the Philippine *peso* is, as the article would put it, as "exotic" as the Indonesian *rupiah* (which yields a fee five times as large, or $2,500 per $1 million handled), Citibank would have exported $1.78 billion.

An official of the Chase Manhattan Bank in New York has confirmed that all major U.S. banks operating in Japan and Southeast Asia lend considerable sums to Japanese companies and Japanese joint ventures. Japanese companies now dominate the investment scene in Southeast Asia; they are number one in Thailand with $160 million, or over 40 percent of total foreign investments, and number one in Indonesia in number of projects with a total investment of $810 million. So we can assume that they are, numerically at least if not in volume, the biggest beneficiaries of these operations. Furthermore, as has been seen, Japanese banks themselves conduct the same genre of profitable operations using local savings. The August, 1975, issue of *Fortune* lists fifteen Japanese banks among the fifty largest commercial banking companies in 1975 outside the United States, five of which were among the first ten. Most of these Japanese banks were operating in Indonesia and Thailand, in the majority of cases in joint ventures with local, European, or U.S. banks, as illustrated in Table 16.

Table 16

Japanese Banks in Indonesia and Thailand as of March, 1975

INDONESIA

Bank	Partner
1. Sanwa	Continental (local)
2. Sumitomo	Export-Import Bank of Indonesia (semi-government)
3. Daiichi Kangyo	Consortium led by Bumi-daya Bank (local)
4. Long Term Credit Bank	Bank of Central Asia (local)
5. Nippon Fudosan Ginko	Consortium led by Bank of Indonesia (government)
6. Fuji	Consortium led by Mutual Promotion, Ltd. (local)
7. Mitsui	Consortium led by Bank Negara Indonesia
8. Mitsubishi	Consortium led by Dagong Negara Bank (local)
9. Bank of Tokyo	No partner

THAILAND

Bank	Partner
1. Daiichi	Two ventures: (1) Thai Farmers' Bank and (2) Siam Commercial Bank and others
2. Tokai	First National City Bank of New York
3. Bank of Tokyo	No partner
4. Sanwa	No partner
5. Fuji	Bangkok Bank of Commerce (local)
6. Mitsui	Consortium: 50% local; 10% European (Commerzbank, Crédit Lyonnais, etc)
7. Mitsubishi	Thai Overseas Trust Co. (local)

Source: Nomura Research Institute, New York.

It is reasonable to assume that these Japanese banks (at least one of them in joint-venture with the First National City Bank), engaged like Citibank in commercial banking, are all competing, in *Fortune*'s phrase, in "raising most of their money in their local markets." In 1973, Kien Theeravit was complaining that most Japanese and Japanese-Thai business firms in Bangkok "open their accounts at either one or both of the Japanese banks" [Tokyo and Mitsui] and that these banks "enjoy equal rights with other local banks which is quite unusual for a foreign bank."[7]The indictment by the president of the Thai Board of Trade would seem to be supported. Falnzylber's picture of Latin America is duplicated quite faithfully in Southeast Asia. The banking expertise and superior resources of the developed nations are utilized to organize local capital. In bidding for this organized capital, the local entrepreneurs with their meager collateral can hardly compete with the giant global enterprises bidding on their own or in joint ventures.

In other words, although the Reserve Bank of Japan stands by with guarantees, the actual money-flow that lubricates the high-loan component, bicycle-action drive of Japanese investment abroad is drawn substantially from the savings of the local population deposited in American, Japanese, and European banks. And since the local partners of the Japanese (mostly Chinese) come from, in Yano's words, "the upper stratum of the dual structure," a good portion of the money of the general population may be said to fuel investments of the Japanese, Chinese, Americans, and those of the population who are already rich. This, again to borrow Yano's phrase, would seem to be anti-revolutionary a priori development par excellence.

In the projections of Japan's Ministry of International Trade and Industry (see Table 9, page 18), by 1985 Japanese overseas investment will be employing 2.9 million people all over the world, including 119,000 Japanese. These impressive figures do not answer the questions: (1) Will they be employed in the kind of industries needed for proper national development, or (2) How many local employees will the industries displace?

With very few exceptions, which we shall cite later, the goal of all Japanese foreign investment, as with most global corporations, is the introduction into the host country of the consumption ethic, the creation of artificial mass desires to justify mass production to justify investment. This ethic, transplanted from developed societies that reached the mass production level without the need of heavy direct foreign investment, is artificially introduced into developing nations whose economies are not ready to meet it. Therefore, the poor country is forced to depend on foreign technology and foreign-organized capital.

Among Indonesian technocrats, the line is fairly well drawn between those who would like to "increase the cake," assured that the division will quite naturally follow (the trickle-down theory), and those who would like to undertake more equitable division now even while the cake is growing. The former are dubbed the Berkeley Mafia, so-called because some of them were educated at Berkeley. In their group are Sadli, Widjojo, Salim, Sumarlin, and Subroto, all

---

[7]Theeravit, *Japanese-Thai Economic Interaction*, p. 369.

well placed in government planning circles. Most of this group were still being trained and were very much out of sight during the Sukarno regime. The second group is identified as the Rotterdam School, composed of somewhat older men like Radius Pramiro, Sumitro Djojohadikusumo, and some lower-echelon men who were essentially trained in Europe. This group, Dr. Frances Starner, political scientist formerly with the *Far Eastern Economic Review*, pointed out in an interview, "have taken serious exception to what they regard as an effort to turn Indonesia into a part of the World Bank-IGGI[8]-IMF structure." They have not "questioned the traditional capitalist world" but have criticized those who have "stressed economic development without regard for social redistribution."

The new government development plan, put together after the anti-Tanaka riots, attempts some "social redistribution" with increased central government subsidies for regional governments and villages and more money for schools, hospitals, and infrastructure. This is a compromise between the two schools, an attempt to hasten the "trickling down" of the benefits from the development at the top. Yet, this may not be what the students had risen for. As early as August, 1973, one Indonesian writer told me, the students had begun openly to demand a change in the whole strategy of economic development.

Two members of the Indonesian Parliament who belonged to the official government GOLKAR party deplored the exclusivism of the Japanese but defended the GNP-oriented development program. At the end of our interview, they made special mention of their dislike for the "huge advertisements of Japanese enterprises" which may have been effective in arousing the students.

Yet, these huge advertisements were, of course, an essential part of the campaign for arousing artificial appetites for the products of the economy in a development strategy geared mainly to growth. In both Jakarta and Bangkok, I was struck by the volume of television advertising for detergents, soft drinks, tooth paste, painkillers—all U.S. and Tokyo (and Manila) style.

The first disillusionment over the consumption ethic came to those Indonesians who discovered that mass production does not necessarily mean mass employment. The greater efficiency of the large foreign investment sector, says the leading intellectual Soedjatmoko, "has tended to drive smaller domestic enterprises off the market, thus aggravating the already serious unemployment problem."[9] The progovernment-newspaper editor, D. H. Assegaff, lamented in an interview that the entrance of Coca Cola (in Indo-

---

[8]Inter-Governmental Group for Indonesia.

[9]Soedjatmoko, Speech delivered at Sophia University Symposium, Tokyo, October 29, 1973.

nesia, a Japanese-Australian joint venture) and large biscuit factories put small-scale industries off the market and more people out of work. He said the baking of bread was, before 1966 (the year Suharto took over), a cottage industry; but with automation it became a large-scale enterprise, putting small bakers out of business. The same is true, he said, of ice cream which used to be turned out by individual small restaurants but is now the monopoly of Australian and even Philippine ("Magnolia") mass-produced brands.

For those Indonesians, added Assegaff, whose taste has not adjusted to the Atlanta tang of Coca Cola and who long nostalgically for something Dutch, there is the soft drink "Fanta" which sells for Rp40 and with which the lowly restaurant tea at Rp75 and local fruit juices cannot compete. (I recall that during the Japanese occupation of the Philippines when we were cut off from our supply of Coca Cola essence, small refreshment stands sprouted up all over the country serving fruit juices made of mango, guava, sampaloc [tamarind], and calamansi [a native lime], stimulating a promising new cottage industry and promoting commercial production of the fruits. All of this was washed away with the first wave of the liberation forces on whose crest rode those voluptuous cola bottles, returning to seduce Filipino tastes all over again.)

No figures have been available to quantify the alleged displacement and disemployment effect of the big Japanese and foreign firms. Panglaykim categorically asserts and other respected pro-government Indonesian technocrats agree that "the introduction of Coca Cola by the Mitsui group and other well-known brands in the soft-drink industry resulted in the closing down of the national beverage industry." In his study of business relations between Indonesia and Japan he adds that "even though some firms have gone into other types of drinks, they still feel the impact of these joint ventures." Furthermore, "severe competition was also felt by national textile firms" which have had either to slow down or close down after attempting to survive by "going into those products not produced by the big textile ventures."[10]

"Certainly we could live without drinking Cocal Cola or smoking foreign-brand filter-tip cigarettes," Minister of Mines Mohammad Sadli told me at his modest but comfortable home in Jarkata (where he served me native coffee), "but it is very difficult. These foreign companies engage in advertising, and because of their advertisement impact they are creating their own demand." Sadli thought that advertising should probably not be encouraged, but that certain realities had to be confronted in that kind of remedy. "Newspapers here are not so widespread," he reflected, "but radio and television in the last five or seven years have been commercialized. Our state-

[10]Panglaykim, *Business Relations*, pp. 41-2.

owned radio and television company needed income to run, so it accepted commercial advertising. That was a compromise with a social price."

An Indonesian intellectual spoke of one pathetic instance of Japanese creating a demand for their products. To stimulate a desire for musical instruments, a Japanese group granted a franchise to a Chinese to organize a music school. When the school had achieved its end, the franchise was withdrawn, and the Chinese reduced to the status of employee.

Sadli thought that the time might come when the national radio and television station would be strong enough not to depend on advertising. "Would you not anticipate opposition from the multinationals if you dropped advertising?" I asked him. "And if the demand is not developed, what then?"

"The market will always develop but maybe not as fast as with advertisement," he replied, "and as the national economy gets stronger there may be no more urgent need for all these multinational companies—they will have served their purpose. The government could then develop a social policy with respect to consumption."

What Sadli was expressing, in fact, was confidence in the eventual success of a government compromise plan which combines all-out consumption-ethic production, trickle-down hopes, and budgetary regional redistribution.

The artificial stimulation of appetites through advertising seemed to be even more blatant in Thailand. "The Japanese people are no worse than other nationals in their desire to sell their goods in the largest quantities," writes the Thai intellectual Kien Theeravit, "but the Japanese have made greater attempts than other nationals and have sometimes used more unscrupulous means than others." The "reduction of presence" by pulling down oversized billboards had been undertaken in Jakarta after the riots but not in Bangkok. "Japan sends plenty of goods to Thailand without considering whether they are to the taste of the Thai people," complains Theeravit, "and resort to changing the tastes of the Thais through the media of advertisements."[11] Chulalongkorn University students lamented that the Thai penchant for extravagance was aggravated by the fact that "most of the luxury items are Japanese products."

Japan Trade Center President Yasuyuki Matsuo observed that "the Anti-Japanese Products Campaign seemed to aim at putting a stop to the importation of luxury goods from Japan." But he pointed out that "90 percent of Thailand's imports from Japan consists of machinery and raw materials necessary for Thailand's industrial development [and that] luxury goods are more or less included, but

---

[11]Theeravit, *Japanese-Thai Economic Interaction*, Chapter 22.

the volume is not enough to make up the trade deficit." Matsuo was singling out the trade balance question because, unlike Indonesia which has managed a consistent trade surplus with Japan mainly because of her oil exports, Thailand considers her trade deficit with Japan a crucial issue.

Matsuo's argument assumes that luxury imports amounting to a maximum, he claims, of 10 percent of the total importation from Japan ($951 million in 1974) is a reasonable "rider" when compared to the volume of machinery and parts imported. The Thais do not seem to agree. Furthermore, the argument also seems to assume that all the Japanese-brand luxury goods consumed in Thailand are imported from Japan. In January, 1975, an article in the *Investor*, a business publication edited by Renoo Suvarnsit, former director of the National Economic and Social Development Board, recalled that the protection-subsidy policies of the Thai Board of Industries (BOI) in the 1960s "provided incentives for Japanese companies in import substitution and were strongly biased against exports." Among the industries that "received high protection [were] passenger car assembly, perfumery, and cosmetics. . . . In contrast," continued the article, "most export industries received negative protection because of the high price of inputs and no direct subsidy of export sales. . . . BOI is very much implicated [in making] import substitution policies work together with the export promotion policies of Japan to create a severely imbalanced trade pattern between the two countries." Among the beneficiaries of such policies are the builders of luxury hotels and the consumers of imported durables such as passenger cars. The article concluded with the hope that the BOI might be able to "redirect investments" but expressed doubts about this possibility, accepting that "it is changes in the structure of the Japanese economy which are more likely to call the tune."

Import substitution resulted in local production of consumer goods, otherwise imported, which may not be directly related to basic development, thus evoking complaints of "extravagance" and "luxury" from militant student groups. Michael Yoshino confirms that "the first target of import substitution was usually the last stage of the production of consumer goods, including the manufacture of textiles or simple metal products, the packaging of drugs and toiletries, and the assembly of consumer durables such as radios, television sets, and refrigerators." Furthermore, the "packaging" and "assembly" character of the operations strengthened the argument for those who thought basic industrialization was not being achieved by the production policy.

But Kun Chada Watanasiritham, economist of the Bank of Thailand, defends assembly operations and warns that "it is not adequate to concentrate on basic industries." Electronic industries in which all the components are imported from abroad and the only Thai contribution is labor "are not basic industries by any means, but they still create employment and earn foreign exchange for us because the products are exported," she explained in an interview.

Franklin Proud of *Business in Thailand* also views the BOI policies with less alarm. He reminded me that BOI-supported activities were mostly those belonging to Thais (although, as we have seen, these would tend to be, in fact, Chinese). He said that about half of foreign investment in Thailand was Japanese and then warned that if, as a result perhaps of the nationalistic trend, foreign investment should withdraw, "then Thai industrial growth will stop."

For some Asian intellectuals, compromise planning and redirection of investments which avoids revising the whole strategy of development of growth for growth's sake is not an acceptable solution to the problem of excessive dependence on foreign investment. Soedjatmoko, who still holds a position as consultant to BAPENAS, the Indonesian Planning Board, argued in his 1973 speech at Sophia University that "primary emphasis on growth is bound to lead to politically and morally unacceptable social discrepancies. . . . The trickle-down theory underlying the traditional concept of economic development has proven to be, both morally and politically, untenable." He warned that "the adoption of consumption patterns and consumption levels of the rich industrial nations by the elite of populous developing nations—before the development of an adequate domestic industrial base of their own and before the proliferation in the countryside of modern technology adapted to the needs and resources of the rural area—is bound to perpetuate, and even increase, dependency from the rich countries, will further depress living standards of the already poor, will widen the gap between the modern elite and society at large, and will distort the optimal allocation of domestic resources for development, again with serious political consequences."

The Indonesian economist Thee Kian-wie, a "pure" technocrat with no political credentials, appeared to agree with the Soedjatmoko analysis. He pointed out in an interview that "the pattern of Japanese investment is geared to the needs of the higher income classes—luxury goods, cars, and so on—aggravating the already unequal distribution of income." He accused the Japanese of "allying themselves with certain officials [and of] making use of certain weaknesses in our administrative structure." Although obviously of Chinese descent himself, Thee lamented the alliance of Japanese "with the Indonesian-Chinese who belong to the higher income classes." Admitting that he was "very controversial," he said he felt Indonesia was not ready to receive "that huge pile of investment from Japan."

Thee recalled that in 1974 he spoke very strongly against Mitsui's intention of investing $1 billion in Indonesia in all kinds of fields. "All that money looked nice," he agreed, "but I felt that in the long run it might be better to have a holding operation first; I mean concentrate to improve our infrastructure rather than on exploitation of our natural resources in cooperation with certain corruptive elements." He admitted that this shift in strategy would not entirely eliminate corruption but he thought it would "at least lead to a strengthening of the infrastructure so that the Indonesians completely control their resources, which is not the case right now.

"Right now, Mitsubishi is conducting a survey of our natural resources," Thee related, "and we do not have such a survey ourselves. Japanese and other foreigners come and say 'Let us conduct a survey,' and then they tell us what our resources are. We do not even know whether they are right or wrong!" (Franklin Proud later told me in Bangkok that "the Japanese know more about Thailand's resources than the Thais [because] during their military occupation of the country in World War II they concentrated on geological exploration.") With their survey in hand, the Japanese, Thee continued, "go to the [provinces] and make their own arrangements with the officials. They know so much about us that we do not know and can foresee consequences of certain actions which we cannot. By the time we do see, we are bound to them for a long time."

Thee admitted that his proposal for "consolidation" before massive foreign investment "might perhaps not lead to a fast rate of growth. . . . But what benefit do you have," he asked, "from a fast rate of growth on paper if in the meantime your country has become like Latin America? Japan's position in Southeast Asia will be just like America's in Latin America—an economic empire built on political quicksand." "We have capital resources, too," he argued, "we could improve on our tax structure, provide the capital ourselves, and go only for management contracts with the Japanese or Europeans."

When I mentioned Thee's observations to Mohammad Sadli, he quickly agreed that Thee had "a point, of course." He thought Thee was probably reflecting the "Mahbub ul Haq type of thinking. He is one of the directors of McNamara's at the World Bank and his populist writings on development approaches are popular among the students here."

Sadli said the Indonesian government "gives cognizance to this more populist, more aggressive type of developmental goal through control of the budget; regional dispersal of infrastructure; education, health, and agriculture support; and through employment-oriented development." But in its promotion of labor-intensive industry, the government seems to be caught in a dilemma. "We cannot regret the growth of the so-called modern capital-intensive sector because it is from that sector where we expect to draw the taxes to be used in the so-called traditional labor-intensive industries," Sadli explained. "We cannot soak the rich because it will probably take some years before we can acquire the well-organized system required for that," he added. "Now we try to soak mainly the foreign oil companies." (Japanese have no significant involvement in Indonesian oil development.)

Sadli's compromise formula seems nowhere near Haq's truly myth-shattering vision. Haq, formerly the chief economist in the Planning Commission of Pakistan and now director of the Policy Planning and Program Review Department of the World Bank, prescribes for the Third World the evolution "of a life style consistent with its own poverty and current level of development rather than pursuing illusive Western living standards, [a development aiming] not merely at the highest rate of GNP growth but at the participation of the majority of the people . . . mobilizing the creative energies of the people themselves, [relying] on local institutions and improvised technology." This new development strategy, suggests Haq, "has to build development around people, rather than people around development and has to achieve this largely through local resources and indigenous effort, [arranging] its own trading patterns based on pots and pans and bicycle economies[12] rather than on the traditional trading patterns between the developing and the developed world."

To permit this new strategy to take effect, Haq exhorts the major creditor and debtor countries to convene a conference to arrange a satisfactory review and settlement of "the $75 billion of debt burden that the Third World has acquired so far as a result of the past so-called foreign assistance." Otherwise, he warns, "new assistance in many of the poor countries is merely paying for old debts and not leading to any significant net transfer of resources."[13]

Haq's warning on "so-called foreign assistance" would douse the enthusiastic response usually elicited by the periodic proud announcements of increased foreign aid by developed nations. The August, 1975, issue of *Fortune* ran a thirty-page paid advertisement entitled, "Japan: Toward Closer Global Communication," which contained a chart showing that "Japan's aid to developing nations" had grown from $485.9 million in 1965 to $5.8 billion in 1973. The advertisement also contained the following paragraph:

> In an effort to strengthen its assistance to developing countries, Japan's central bank recently agreed to lend $100 million to the Manila-based Asian Development Bank [ADB], which is a prime source of financing for developing countries in Asia. It will be the first loan by the Japanese to the bank and it underscores Japan's increasing involvement in ADB, which is currently headed by a Japanese.

We saw in Chapter 3 that Japan now lays claim to being the

---

[12]I.e., real bicycles, not to be confused with the head-long bicycle action of the Japanese economy.

[13]Mahbub ul Haq, Keynote address, Dag Hammarskjold Foundation Seminar (Stockholm, 1973).

biggest annual lender to the World Bank itself, supplying 24.9 percent of the Bank's world borrowings in fiscal year 1974. Presumably, Haq includes loans from the World Bank among those forms of foreign assistance that have created the astronomical debt burden for the Third World.

Japan's upcoming $100-million loan to the Asian Development Bank may further strengthen its already pronounced influence on the decisions of ADB. In 1971, Takeshi Watanabe, then the bank's president, admitted, according to the *Washington Post*, that "out of $50 million disbursed by the bank up to April, 1971, $30.6 million had gone to procurement in Japan." As for bilateral Japanese aid, the popular belief that it is conducted largely for export promotion seems to be substantiated by the facts. Kien Theeravit recalls that the two big long-term loans given by Japan to Thailand of (baht) B1.2 billion in 1968 and B4.5 billion in 1972 (about $60 million and $225 million at current rates) were at high interest rates ranging up to or over 5 percent and "required imported goods and services to come from Japan."[14] According to the *Washington Post* (February 25, 1973), of the $1.267 billion in "aid" to Asia in 1971, $837 million consisted of export and investment credits at interest rates of 6 to 8 percent.

Some Japanese have been critical of their aid program. Governor Nagasu has analyzed Japanese aid as "a pie which slices three ways: (A) government loans, (B) government and private export credits, and (C) direct investment by private corporations. Category C," he explains, "is of course overseas expansion of Japanese business and not aid. A and B types, particularly B which is far greater, usually go not to another country but to a Japanese company." The result of this deceptively labeled program is, as he puts it, that "the products and the debts from the loans go out of Japan, [the aid] stimulates the production capacity of Japanese companies more than those in the recipient areas [and results in] unbalanced trade patterns."[15] Ambassador Fujizaki in Bangkok, displaying a scholarly and open mind, admitted his regret that even one-year deferred payments for equipment from Japan were counted as aid. In this light, the advertised figure of $5.8 billion in Japanese aid to developing nations might perhaps be viewed with somewhat less awe.

The *Fortune* advertisement points, perhaps with justifiable pride, to such recent economic assistance items as $85 million in loans for South Korean agricultural and port development, $35 million in credit for an Indian fertilizer plant, $40 million for Indonesian power plant and radio network projects, and $30 million for Singapore's electric supply facilities.

---

[14]Threeravit, *Japanese-Thai Economic Interaction*, p. 366.

[15]Nagasu, "Super-Illusions of an Economic Superpower," p. 154.

Furthermore, the long-delayed Asahan hydroelectric and aluminum smelter complex, a key project in the Indonesian development scheme, is finally on the way to construction with the conclusion of an agreement (concluded in July, 1975, to coincide with President Suharto's visit to Tokyo), in which the Japanese government will put up 70 percent of the $845 million total cost; private Japanese banks, 20 percent; and the Indonesian government, 10 percent. A 426,000-kilowatt electric power plant will be constructed on the upper reaches of the Asahan River in northeastern Sumatra, and a 247,500-ton-a-year aluminum smelter will be built near the coastal town of Kuala Tandjung. Twelve Japanese companies will own 90 percent of the smelter, and the Indonesian government will own 10 percent. Indonesia will fully own the power plant from the start and the smelter after thirty years.

The agreement was hailed in the July 8, 1975, London *Financial Times* as appearing "to mark a decisive close to the unhappy period in Japan-Indonesian relations which followed Prime Minister Tanaka's visit to Jakarta in January, 1974." Yet, a few questions seem to remain unanswered, not only on the Asahan project but also on those economic assistance projects in India, South Korea, and Singapore: What are the conditions of the loans? Will the consequent burden of repayment be bearable by a society that must compromise with the consumer ethic; or will it, as Mahbub ul Haq has warned, create societies unable to pursue future policies because of the burdens of the past? In the thirty years that Indonesia will be waiting fully to own the aluminum smelter, can it achieve a more equitable distribution of wealth while satisfying stimulated wants so that there is no recurrence of violent rioting?

"The next three years will be critical," forecasts one Indonesian. "The problem will not go away until it is tackled and development goals are redefined. If they are not, we may have rioting again."

VIII

Collision

In 1973-74, the "antirevolutionary" Japanese presence was a significant factor in two uprisings in Southeast Asia. One succeeded in bringing down a dictatorial government; the other did not. In both cases, there is evidence that to some extent the Japanese were victims of "scapegoating" by various sides, e.g., the students, opposing factions of the army, the political opposition, the government itself. "This is partly correct," admits Governor Nagasu, "but it would be a mistake to conclude that Japan is simply being used as a convenient scapegoat."[1]

If the desirability, character, and quality of Japanese investment in Thailand and Indonesia are not quickly assessable, the quantity and size are of such obvious proportions that they could lend themselves to scapegoating. In Thailand, Japan accounted for 41.57 percent of the total foreign registered capital as of December 31, 1974. The United States was a poor second with 14.54 percent. By June 30, 1974, eighty-three Japanese firms were in operation with thirty-one more approved but not yet operating.[2] In Indonesia, the United States leads foreign investors in dollar terms, but the Japanese lead in the number of projects. Even in dollar terms, Japan's presence is impressive. Of the $3.5 billion in Japanese overseas investment in 1972-73, $405 million was in Indonesia, mostly in resource-oriented activities intended to insure continued supplies of raw materials. Of the sixteen top global corporations operating in Indonesia in 1973, ten were Japanese handling a combined total of sixty-nine projects, two were American with three projects, two Dutch with two projects, and two German with two projects.[3] By

---

[1]Nagasu, "Super-Illusions of an Economic Superpower," p. 162.

[2]Statistics from the Thai Board of Investments, Bangkok.

[3]Statistics from the Centre for Strategic and International Studies, Jakarta.

January, 1975, as mentioned earlier, Japan had invested $810 million in Indonesia and $160 million in Thailand.

In September, 1972, Thai Lieutenant Colonel Narong Kittikachorn, son of then Premier Thanom Kittikachorn, along with his father and his father-in-law, General Prapat Charusatien (the ruling triumvirate), denounced, in his capacity as chairman of the Corruption Suppression Committee, Japan's "unashamed policy of economic imperialism in Thailand." The following November, the government officially supported (some say inspired) a ten-day boycott of Japanese goods led by student organizers. A few days before the boycott, customs officials announced the imposition of almost a million dollars in fines on six Japanese trading firms for falsifying declarations. The orchestration included a preboycott campaign by progovernment newspapers.

The boycott urged the Thais not to patronize Japanese goods, eat in Japanese restaurants, or fly on Japan Air Lines. It called for elimination of strings on Japanese aid and the improvement of the negative trade balance. Sporadic violence erupted, with student factions brandishing screwdrivers at local Japanese. In December, students attacked the Japanese-owned Daimaru department store. There were suspicions that the attack was instigated by rival Thai-Chinese department stores. As has been mentioned, sons of rich Thai-Chinese were reportedly seen among the attackers.

The triumvirate had not been thorough in its repression and, by contrast with the suppression of the Philippine press, the newspapers in Thailand were relatively free. The *Bangkok Post*, for instance, was allowed to retain its British-style independence. In 1972, it exposed the "hunting scandal" involving generals, including Prapat, who controlled huge game preserves where they hunted with the use of army helicopters.

The Thai press apparently kept the people fairly well informed of corruption among the generals, including the triumvirate, most particularly Narong. If Narong, indeed, had used the Japanese as a scapegoat, his tactic was soon to boomerang. A Thai journalist recalled that Narong was soon singled out by the people because he was "very arrogant," a charge Narong himself had hurled at the Japanese. Prapat was directly linked to Japanese corruption.

The students who had flexed their muscles in the anti-Japanese action were now finding themselves ready to turn against the government. By June, 1973, they had developed mass protests against "law breakers," demanding action against corruption and the early proclamation of a constitution which the triumvirate had been promising but constantly postponing. The arrest of about a dozen students for petitioning for a constitution provoked a demonstration in October which proved to be decisive. The university students were joined by vocational students, workers, and the ordinary people of Bangkok. At the peak, the unarmed marchers were reported to have numbered over a quarter of a million. The BIFCO, Narong's private office building, was burned whereupon Narong went up in an aircraft and began to fire (blank bullets, it was discovered later) at the marchers, further incensing them. Elements of the military and police fired on the marchers, killing sixty-five. (Some observers like Sanan Vong-suthee, one of the few Thais who have developed into authentic labor leaders under the laws which have made unionism difficult, would stress the importance of the participation of the workers. Sanan claimed in an interview that when the firing came there were more workers than students at the vanguard of the march.)

General Krit Srivara, the newly appointed commander in chief, rejected General Prapat's command to crush the march—now turned into a revolt—by force. The king supported Krit's decision, disavowed the triumvirate who were allowed to flee the country, and called on an obscure but respected university professor, Sanya Dharmasakti, to lead a provisional government that was to draft a new democratic constitution and hold elections within a year.

In the euphoria of freedom regained, the Japanese issue might have been temporarily forgotten even by the student movement with its new-found power. But Prime Minister Tanaka chose that moment to drop in for a visit.

Foreign correspondents, like Thomas Pepper of the *Baltimore Sun*, commented on the eve of Tanaka's ten-day goodwill trip to the five ASEAN nations which began on January 7, 1974, that the premier was facing cheers and jeers from his hosts. As we shall see, the odds, particularly in Indonesia, seemed heavily to favor the jeers. But these very odds seem to have been taken by Tanaka as a challenge, and, despite an ear infection which gave him a swollen cheek, he pushed ahead with his plan "to prove to these countries," said Gaimusho ("Foreign Ministry") sources, "that Japan is not trying to dominate them politically or economically." Displaying optimism and self-confidence, he agreed in advance to meet personally with a group of Thai students who had participated in earlier demonstrations against the Japanese.

Tanaka had perhaps hoped that a dispassionate dialogue, which an official of the Japanese embassy in Bangkok had personally organized, would satisfy the students who were itching for an encounter with him. But upon Tanaka's arrival in Bangkok, thousands of students, this time with no evident government instigation or "scapegoating" (the new government was just beginning to organize the return to democracy), descended upon his hotel, the Erawan. From noon until late evening, they roared their English chants ("Jap, go home!") and displayed their English placards ("Don't exploit Thailand"; "We don't want any Japanese tricks"; "Tanaka, how can I love you?").

The next day, Tanaka met with a delegation of thirteen students led by Sombat Thamrongthanyawongse, secretary-general of the

National Student Center which had been mainly resonsible for organizing the decisive demonstration that overthrew the triumvirate. They presented a letter denouncing Japanese trade and investment that favored only Japan, Japanese "exploitation" of Thai labor, and self-serving Japanese aid. Tanaka listened with all "respect and with an unbiased heart," as he later told newsmen, but made no specific commitments. The students, as someone later observed of their Indonesian counterparts, had apparently not done their homework too well, judging from their vague answers to searching questions by the press asking for detailed evidence to support their charges. But they had accomplished the rare feat of direct confrontation with a visiting head of state who otherwise would have confined himself to traditional political and diplomatic channels.

If Tanaka's reception in Bangkok was not as shocking and violent as that which was to meet him in Jakarta, it might have been because violence had just reached its high point in Thailand. A dictatorship had just been toppled, and the demonstration against Tanaka was therefore "purer" since it was staged as the exercise of regained liberties and not as a step to recover lost ones. There was no longer a corrupt ruling family to protest against. The new, and provisional, government was to be "given a chance." The demonstration was purely anti-Japanese, and nobody could cry "scapegoating!" Tanaka could find no more consolation there than in Manila which, as Nagasu observes, "is under martial law, and even if there was discontent the people could not publicly express it"[4]; or in Kuala Lumpur, where, in spite of a ban on mass demonstrations, about fifty students would meet him at the airport accusing him of seeking to "consolidate the position of Japanese economic exploiters in the country"; or in Singapore, where Lee Kwan-yew is known to run a tight ship and not to brook any disturbances.

Unmistakable indications that the reception in Jakarta would be violent had been mounting and had been reported in the Japanese press for a month before the visit. On December 1, 1973, the *Japan Times* carried an Associated Press report that University of Indonesia students had marched to the Japanese embassy to demand that Japan stop its production of synthetic rubber or "get out of Indonesia." On December 11, *Yomiuri* reported a youth demonstration "atop and inside a Japanese-built thirty-story building in Jakarta." On December 12, both *Yomiuri* and the *Japan Times* headlined the arrest of Indonesian youths who had marched to the building of the Tokyo Astra Motors, a Japanese-Indonesian company, to protest what they called exhibition of powerful foreign capital in Indonesia. On December 14, *Mainichi* said the Agence France-Presse had reported that in Jakarta "security and military commanders warned student leaders that unceasing demonstrations were taxing their patience and dangerously bordering on crime."

---

[4]Nagasu, "Super-Illusions of an Economic Superpower," p. 150.

On December 20, *Mainichi* reported that University of Indonesia student council chairman Harriman Sinegar had been asked to resign by his fellow council members for not consulting them on the decision to "demonstrate against Prime Minister Kakuei Tanaka when he arrives here next month." On December 22, the same paper carried a Kyodo (Japanese) News Agency report that Toyota Motor, the largest automaker in Japan, "began to dismantle its advertisement neon sign set up on the . . . highest building here." On December 28, the *Japan Times* published a combined Kyodo-Reuters report that "students in Indonesia are preparing to take unspecified action against the forthcoming visit of Prime Minister Kakuei Tanaka" according to student leader Harriman Sinegar. On December 29, the *Asahi Evening News* reported an appeal by the Indonesian government to students "not to demonstrate against Prime Minister Tanaka in mid-January [because] being an oriental nation, as a host, we should welcome our guest respectfully." Finally, on January 13, 1975, two days before Tanaka's arrival in Jakarta, the *Japan Times* put out another Kyodo-Reuters report which warned that anti-Japanese sentiment was mounting as Tanaka's visit drew closer, citing students at the Indonesian Christian University who had burned him in effigy on their campus.

In spite of these warning signs which seemed alarming enough in print, the advance party, which had been in Jakarta since early January to prepare for the visit, gave Tanaka the final all-clear signal. Toru Yano, a member of the advance party, recalled that they had considered the December and early January incidents as "a series of petty student demonstrations." He himself had thought that the riots that ensued after Tanaka's arrival were staged by a faction of the military. But the advance party, which included police intelligence officers from Tokyo, had apparently been deceived by such happenings as the one on January 2 when two generals known to be rivals for power under Suharto appeared together and shook hands before newspaper reporters, denying the rampant rumors that they were headed for a showdown. "The Indonesian government insisted on the visit as scheduled and gave us no hint of what might happen," Yano said in an interview. "We had no reason to refuse; it was a sort of diplomatic inevitability."

Tanaka may not have realized as he flew to Jakarta that he was about to step into a convoluted situation which only someone with a historical perspective of the Indonesian student movement could have begun to understand. In postwar Southeast Asia, it is the Thai and Indonesian students who have displayed the most consistent mutual rapport. The Bangkok universities had watched with avid interest the tactics of the Indonesian students in bringing down Sukarno in 1966. These lessons were applied successfully in the October, 1973, uprising against the Thai dictatorship. Now the lesson-learning was about to come full circle. The Indonesian students, apparently stimulated by the success of their Thai colleagues, began their own mass actions in Jakarta, fired by the Indonesian press which, like the Thai newspapers under the triumvirate, was allowed surprising, though relative, freedom by the Suharto government. Only a few days after the Thai uprising, the students of the University of Indonesia came out with the Petition of 24th October protesting corruption, abuse of authority, rising prices and unemployment, and calling for a review of the lopsided strategy of development. Next, they took advantage of the visit on November 11 of the Dutch minister for development cooperation, Jan P. Pronk (who ironically is one of those in the Western world most sympathetic to developing nations), to declare, "We do not take pride in the results of foreign aid and foreign capital in the form of tall buildings, Coca Cola, nightclubs, etc., while our people are without jobs, homes and land, our small textile industry has died, our forests have become barren and our oil fields depleted." Subsequently, they visited government leaders to protest policies on foreign capital and conspicuous consumption and demonstrated at the hotel where the Miss Indonesia beauty contest was being held. As the Tanaka visit approached, the actions turned increasingly against the Japanese, and we have seen how they were reported even in the Japanese press.

The military power structure which the students seemed to be defying regarded the demonstrations with mixed feelings of concern and, it is said, of opportunity. The main target was the Aspri, the supercabinet group of presidential assistants, most prominent of whom were Major General Ali Moertopo and Major General Sudjono Humardhani, respectively branded in the press as "Kingmaker" and "Rasputin." The two were "exposed" in newspapers like *Pedoman* and *Indonesia Raya* (both suppressed since the riots) for alleged Japanese business involvements. Many officers in the active service were said to resent the pre-eminence of the Aspri and the business activities of some of them which seemed to be leading to student and peasant unrest. General Panggabean, the commander of the armed forces, was close to the Aspri, but his deputy, General Sumitro, who also held the powerful post of commander of the Kopkamtib ("security forces"), was increasingly recognized as the spokesman of the anti-Aspri "professionals."

Eventually, Moertopo and Sumitro emerged as the main protagonists in the power struggle, and Suharto was hard put to maintain them in balance. Meanwhile, the modern manufacturing sector had become identified as the preserve of Japanese/overseas-Chinese/Indonesian military joint ventures operating in a development plan that did not seem to begin to solve the problems of poverty and unemployment but was producing a class of predominantly Indonesian military and Chinese capitalists devoted to lavish consumption. This development and Japanese "visibility"

(U.S. investment was concentrated in outlying areas) produced a condition that was threatening to explode in three directions.

There had already been, as we have seen, anti-Chinese rioting in Bandung in August, 1973. The government had tried to blame that on the underground communists. Yet, two lieutenant colonels and several other officers of the army's Siliwangi division were arrested along with several civilian leaders of the army-sponsored Angkatan Muda Siliwangi ("Siliwangi Youth Wing"). Ethnic Sundanese in the division had apparently supported the rioting to protest government policies favoring Chinese and foreign investors.

The next month, Muslim students swarmed onto the floor of the parliament during the discussion of a bill that would secularize marriage rules, by tradition heavily influenced by Muslim customs, which had been under heavy attack from women's organizations fighting for more protection and women's rights. The origin and inspiration for the bill had been traced to Moertopo's office.

Sumitro used these two issues to project himself as an alternative to the Aspri. He held back on antistudent reprisals, visited campuses and promised "two-way communication," and, in consultation with Muslim leaders, drafted a new marriage bill which finally was enacted into law. Suharto sensed the intensity of the power struggle and called Moertopo and Sumitro to an amity meeting which resulted in the two making the joint press appearance on January 2 which seems to have strengthened the confidence of Toru Yano and the Japanese advance party. But, perhaps without Yano and the Indonesian officials realizing it, Sumitro apparently continued to attempt to consolidate his position in the ensuing days, meeting with the conservative retired General Nasution (a central figure in the overthrow of Sukarno) and officials of the Military Academy. It soon became known that Suharto had, in fact, reprimanded Sumitro on January 2, and it was rumored that Sumitro might be dismissed after the crisis.

Days before Tanaka's arrival on January 14, unrestrained students burned effigies of Tanaka and Humardhani in Jakarta and Bandung and demonstrated in front of Moertopo's office. When Tanaka arrived, thousands of students paraded in the streets demanding the dissolution of the Aspri and an end to high prices and corruption. By afternoon, the marchers had been joined by youths from the poorer sections of the city, and the march quickly turned into a riot. The rioters burned Japanese cars, including those in showrooms; damaged more than 50,000 stores, mostly owned by Chinese; set fire to 114 buildings; built bonfires with furniture tossed out of Japanese offices; and attacked the Coca Cola plant and the big Senen shopping complex. Among other targets were Japanese-style massage parlors (considered offensive by conservative Muslims) and the Japanese-owned President Hotel, whose management was forced to haul down the Japanese flag. On the second day, troops fired on and killed about a dozen apparent looters at the Senen complex.

But throughout most of the rioting, "the police forces did not function at all," Yano complained, "they simply let things go on; their pretext was that they couldn't shoot anybody when there was an official visitor. This, Yano told me, "made some people smell that that there was a sort of political drama going on behind."

Some of the drama seemed to come out from behind when Sumitro himself was seen on the hood of a jeep on the first day of the demonstration addressing students in far-from-belligerent tones in front of the Japanese embassy. After expressing admiration for their ideals but cautioning them not to burn any more cars, he drove away reportedly to the cheers of the crowd. Tanaka himself was asked to stay at Merdeka Palace throughout his visit while officials apologized to him and made explanations to the press. The foreign minister, Adam Malik—who was apparently not identified with any of the factions in the power struggle—perhaps to soothe the visiting Japanese, told the press that not only Japanese economic policies but also anti-Chinese and anticorruption sentiments were the reasons for the violence of the first day. He affirmed that Japanese were paying bribes and kickbacks but said corruption in Indonesia was "everywhere."

Tanaka was airlifted by helicopter from the palace for his departure after he had assured his hosts and the press that he was not "perturbed or annoyed" by the disturbances which were of the same kind that had occurred in Japan, the United States, and other countries. In Tokyo, he was met with public criticism ranging from failure to assess the extent of anti-Japanese feeling in Asia to charges from the Socialists of "economic intrusion" and "great-nation chauvinism" and from the Communists of "neocolonialistic economics." Tanaka invited his badly shaken countrymen in a Diet speech "to give ear humbly to reasonable criticisms against Japan, correct what we can correct, and improve our mutual relationships with a long-range perspective."

The open recrimination, debate, and assessment that followed Tanaka's return to Tokyo was in contrast to the tense whispering which he had left behind in Jakarta where answers were being sought to questions like: Who started it all? Who was the real scapegoat? Had the students really intended to be violent? Suharto acted by placing a piece of the blame on almost everyone who could be suspected. Sumitro, only forty-eight, was retired after he was reported to have declined an appointment as ambassador to Washington. His other allies accepted foreign assignments or safe army desk jobs. On the other hand, the Aspri was dissolved, and Moertopo apparently was removed from the president's side. His magazine, *Pop*, which had published an article about Suharto's family history which the latter had resented, was suppressed along with Mochtar Lubis's

Indonesia Raya and Rosihan Anwar's *Pedoman*. But Moertopo seemed too firmly entrenched in various established institutions to be totally eliminated. When I arrived in Jakarta a year after the riots, he had just left for the OPEC meeting in Algiers as a member of the official Indonesian delegation headed by Malik, having reportedly impressed Suharto with his command of oil statistics, supplied by his Centre for Strategic and International Studies. It was also rumored that he might be appointed minister of home affairs. There were further strong reports of a reconciliation between Suharto and Sumitro, with Suharto consenting to be sponsor at Sumitro's wedding.

While Suharto was striving mightily to avoid a violent break with any of the suspected power seekers in the army, the military leaders had started to blame the riotings on the old PSI (Socialist party) which Sukarno had banned in 1960. The student leader Harriman Sinegar was accused of PSI connections, tried, and sentenced to six years imprisonment. Other former PSI leaders, like Subadio and Professor Sarbini, Sinegar's father-in-law, were arrested. While I was in Jakarta, Schachrir, another student leader, was undergoing trial.

A Western diplomat in Jakarta told me observers were finding it hard to believe that the Socialists had influenced the students into rioting. A credible Indonesian source who requested anonymity was certain that the violence had been launched by hired men of Moertopo, claiming that there was evidence to this effect in the hands of the attorney general's office and the BAKIN ("Army Intelligence"). Others asked, "Did Sumitro's plan of unleashing the students really backfire when violence exploded, or was Sumitro himself responsible for the violence?" Japanese embassy officials recalled that "a lot of the demonstrators came in trucks and buses" and wondered who had supplied or paid for the ride.

It may take considerable time before history succeeds in sorting out the instigators from the scapegoats. In the meantime, can it happen again? The progovernment editor D. H. Assegaff was certain "there would be no demonstrations within five years," apparently pinning his hopes on the success of the government's five-year social redistribution plan. Jacob Utomo, editor of the Catholic paper *Kompas*, thought there would be no more demonstrations "if the Japanese correct their corruption and the government promotes regulations to control them." Japanese embassy officials, on the other hand, thought the possibility of new riots would depend on the policies and performance of the government. "This year's budget is inflationary," one of them told me. "If it satisfies the masses, O.K.; but if only rich people are benefited. . . . " Panglaykim, who was certain that the riots were not really anti-Japanese but were used "as a rallying force to down the government and introduce a socialist strategy of development," thought that the Japanese issue could not provoke future riots because "the Japanese are now rather restrained, perhaps because of their tight money policy, and have changed their strategy into one of going into partnership with the government." One Indonesian intellectual, otherwise critical of Japanese policies, felt that "the mood in Indonesia has changed; the recession in Japan has caused Indonesian fears to recede."

Yet, Japan is over its tight money policy and is the first industrial country to arrest recessionary tendencies. It is in fact facing a labor shortage. So another Indonesian intellectual predicts "trouble from now to five years if the present generals continue to work closely with Japanese interests." Australian scholar Harold Crouch of the Centre of Southeast Asian Studies at Monash University fears that "as long as the Suharto regime permits the private commercial interests of its members and supporters to stand in the way of significant reform, it can be expected that opposition within the army will grow while the failure of the government to reduce civilian alienation will again provide opportunities for dissident officers to move against the government."

Derek Davies disagreed with this pessimism in an interview. He thinks that both Indonesia and Thailand "have gotten rid of the trauma or shocked themselves with what happened as a result of the riots." Malaysia, he admitted, "could be a potential [trouble] spot because it has not happened there, and where it has happened they have rather learned their lesson." Davies's view was challenged by his former colleague, Dr. Frances Starner. Starner agreed that "it could happen in Malaysia" but felt it could also happen again in Indonesia. "Part of Derek's optimism," she said in Jakarta, "may be based on the fact that the leaders of the student movement have been incarcerated, but I certainly would think that if times get any worse in Indonesia—and that is a possibility—you don't need the student leadership to get some kind of riots going."

It may take a fundamental change in development strategy, which will probably be resisted by the developed nations, before developing nations like Indonesia and Thailand can keep their social and economic conditions from deteriorating. In 1973, the average per capita income in the developing countries was $180, compared with $2,400, the average for developed nations. World Bank sources predict that, by 1980, unless revolutionary changes are introduced in the relationships between poor and rich nations as well as in the internal development strategies of the poor ones, this gap will widen to $3,230. Frustrated expectations in Indonesia could be further aggravated by the realization that Indonesian per capita income is $90, one -half the average of poor nations, while in 1980, a mere four years from now, Japan's GNP will be $2,274 billion or $12,490 per capita. The Indonesian government per capita GNP projection for 1974-75 was $145. Of the working Indonesian population, 30 percent is either underemployed or unemployed, and one million more people enter the labor market each year.

The absence of effective safety valves of self-expression could produce more violent manifestations of this frustration in the future. The relative freedom which the Indonesian press had enjoyed in the pre-Tanaka-riot period was severely curtailed in the blame-searching after Tanaka's departure, with the more important independent newspapers suppressed. Thousands of political prisoners are still kept in island stockades. The trial and imprisonment of student leaders appears to have silenced the student population, but the continuing activism of their successful counterparts in Thailand may inspire them to new demonstrations in the face of an unimproved economic situation.

The democracy that the students and workers helped to restore to Thailand has bred confidence that anti-Japanese feelings will be aired in more parliamentary modes. We have noted the much less violent character of the anti-Tanaka reception in Bangkok, which came as an anticlimax after the successful popular march against the dictatorship only three months before. Another military coup is always a possibility, but earlier dire predictions in 1974 appear to have been belied by the continued survival of Kukrit Pramoj's government and the successful, if somewhat violent elections in April, 1976, which put Kukrit's brother, Seni, in power. Most Thai and Japanese observers agree with Kazuko Tomita's prediction that if the Thai army decided to take over again "they would have to kill many more people."

To Somsakdi Xuto, rector of the National Institute of Development and professor of International Relations in Bangkok, "the meaning of the successful October, 1973, peaceful march against the dictatorship was this: that we Thais are just human beings and there are some things we cannot tolerate." Xuto, who was the chief commentator on radio and television during the elections that followed the fall of the triumvirate, said in an interview that he felt the elections had refuted the cynicism of some Thais, "including politicians," who had expressed doubts on the capacity of many of the Thais who were not educated to pass judgment on elected representatives. "We threw about three-fourths of the old politicians out in the last election," he said, "even though money was thrown into the campaign like hell." Dr. Narongchai Akraraseranee, young economist at Thammasat University, observed in an interview in January, 1975, that although "at the moment the democratic government does not seem to be working too efficiently to most of the observers, the students generally feel that this is better than the other alternative." Yoshio Murakami, *Asahi* correspondent in Bangkok, admitted in an interview that when the students raised the issue of "how corrupt the old regime was, they were referring to the connection with Japanese business," but he observed that "today everything is very quiet."

In any case, says Starner, much depends "on the long-term effects of the recession that has hit Japan." Press reports in late 1975 on the number of company bankruptcies in Japan that are blamed on the recession have projected a bleak picture of the future prospects of the Japanese economy. But an analysis of the record of Japanese bankruptcies compared to those among U.S. companies might evoke less pessimism. Of 2,591,000 U.S. concerns in business in 1974, 9,915 (about 0.38 percent) went bankrupt. The average liability of the failures was $307,931. In the same year, 11,691 Japanese firms failed, with an average liability of Y10 million ($300,000). No figures are available on the total number of firms in operation, but a Nomura Research Institute source estimated that the failures represented from 0.2 percent to 0.4 percent of the total, or possibly a slightly lesser percentage than the U.S. casualties. But the Nomura source stressed that what was more meaningful was the increase of bankruptcies over the 1973 figure of 8,202, a jump of 42.4 percent. The U.S. increase over the 1973 figure of 9,345 is negligible.

Yet, the Japanese figures for the first semester of 1975 (4,555) compared to those of the second semester of 1974 (6,055) seem to indicate that the Japanese planners have succeeded in bringing down the rate of bankruptcies. Furthermore, a look at pre-recession statistics shows that Japanese firm failures have been oscillating between eight and ten thousand per annum. In 1968, at the height of the boom, there were 10,776 failures, dropping to 8,253 in 1969 and rising to 9,765 in 1970. The same pattern is seen in the U.S. performance of 9,636 in 1968, 9,154 in 1969, and 10,748 in 1970.[5]

In September, 1975, Deputy Prime Minister Takeo Fukuda, who is concurrently director-general of the Economic Planning Agency, officially informed Japanese business leaders that inflation had become of secondary importance since consumer price rises, already declining, would slow down to a single-digit annual rate by the next month. This meant that the tight money policy was officially over and plant operations, then running at 76 to 80 percent of capacity, would be boosted all over the country. According to the *Journal of Commerce* (September 16, 1975), Fukuda predicted a net growth rate of 5 percent in the second half of fiscal year 1975 (October, 1975, to March, 1976) which would contrast dramatically with the then expansion rate of slightly above zero.

When the usually self-deprecating Japanese make an optimistic prediction, one has to take it seriously. The vertical *ie* is once more showing its resilience and versatility. The Tokyo Express is still on the rails—and very much on course. And more collisions still loom ahead.

---

[5] U.S. bankruptcy statistics (1968-73) are taken from *The Statistical Abstract of the United States: 1974* (Washington, D.C.: United States Bureau of the Census, 1974).

IX

Change from Within?

Dialogue and Cooperation

There are those within the system who would like to change it in order that, as Takeo Miki said upon becoming prime minister in December, 1974, Japan might "enjoy a sense of trust by the rest of the world."

Kazushige Hirazawa, distinguished journalist and close advisor to Miki, said in an interview in Tokyo in January, 1975, that the new government would seek "a common language [and] strive for a more psychological, more cultural, more human rapport" with Southeast Asia. "Miki's approach," said Hirazawa, "is that of dialogue and cooperation." Japanese aid would be tailored to that most appreciated by the recipient people. There is a laudable touch of the people-to-people concept in this approach which would be an improvement on the over-the-people activities of Japanese business. The board chairman of Nissan Motors, for instance, expressed sincere shock at the Jakarta riots since "as far as we could tell from our contacts with Southeast Asian businessmen, relations were quite amicable and government officials also appreciate our presence because it helps them to develop their automobile industries." Penetrating to the "local people" through the curtain of official receptions and lavish businessmen's dinners would provide the Japanese with a deeper insight into the real needs and wants of the people. But this is not easy to do in most of Southeast Asia where, as Nagasu puts it, "the distance between the authorities and the people has been accentuated by periods of martial law or military rule, as in Thailand until last year and Indonesia and the Philippines at present."[1]

The next best thing is to reorganize the aid program in accordance with existing evidence of complaints and suggestions from

---

[1]Nagasu, "Super-Illusions of an Economic Superpower," p.151.

98

the recipient countries. Upon assuming office, Miki appointed Saburo Ohkita; former Undersecretary of Foreign Affairs Shinsaku Hogen, now president of Japan International Cooperation Agency; and Satoshi Sumita, president of the Export-Import Bank, all of whom I interviewed in Tokyo, to plan the "streamlining of the mechanism" of foreign aid, the improvement of loan conditions, and the increase of grants. Their planning has apparently reached the point of being translated into official policy but is generating the expected bureaucratic debate. In July, 1975, the Japanese-language *Nihon Keizai* reported that "in view of the fact that there is strong criticism overseas that 'the terms of Japan's aid are too severe,' the Foreign Ministry is taking the policy of devoting utmost efforts to improve the quality of the Government's development aid." This is to be done, the report said, by (1) increasing the ratio of nonreimbursible aid (i.e., grants) and (2) establishing easy standard terms for yen loans and supplying yen loans on this basis. However, the report added, "the Finance Ministry is showing objections, on the grounds of its increasing the financial burden." The report then went on candidly to admit that although Japanese aid was the fourth in quantity, "in point of quality it is the worst among main advanced nations."

In Japan's total aid, the ratio of grants is 27 percent. In U.S. aid, it is 72 percent; in the case of France, it is 80 percent; and West Germany, 51 percent. Japanese interest rates average 3.5 percent with a repayment period of 23.5 years. U.S. loans are at an average of 2.6 percent interest with a repayment period of 38 years. The Foreign Ministry would like to increase the grants from the current Y15.7 billion to more than Y20 billion in 1976. It would also like to match U.S. interest rates and repayment periods.

In view of Finance ministry objections, the *Nihon Keizai* reported, the matter will be thrown to the Consultative Conference of Cabinet Members connected with overseas economic cooperation. There Miki will find the setting for the exercise of leadership. When he paid his ceremonial visit at the Ise Shrine, upon assuming office, he declared that he would, in Hirazawa's words, "ask the Japanese people to get rid of the idea of going back to the high rate of living." There he was asking the people to tighten their belts a bit in order not only to adjust to the recession, now apparently under control, but also to enable Japan to meet what the Foreign Ministry calls "expenses for international obligation." According to Hirazawa, he will have to intensify his dialogue with labor and with the people at large, telling them that they must change the "orbit of their economic law." Presumably, Miki will support the Foreign Ministry proposals at the Consultative Conference.

Code of Behavior

What Miki cannot claim credit for is something that has yet to prove its worth—the much-discussed nine-point Code of Behavior.

This code was drafted by Japanese business organizations in June, 1973, too close to the Tanaka state visits of January, 1974, to assess its relevance to the violent demonstrations. "We have had so many codes of conduct for businessmen in our history," Toru Yano said in Kyoto. "I have discovered a very interesting one coded as early as 1869." (On February 22, 1869, just thirteen months after Emperor Mutsuhito had decreed the abolition of the Tokugawa *Shogunate* and begun the Meiji Restoration, the Tsushoshi ["Office of Trade"] issued "Guidelines on the Conduct of Business Abroad.")

The 1973 Code of Behavior was urged upon Japanese business by the Ministry of Foreign Affairs, whose missions abroad had been reporting increasing signs of anti-Japanese feeling. Officially titled "Guidelines for Investments in Developing Countries," the code was formulated by five organizations: the Keidanren (the big business groups), the Japanese Chamber of Commerce and Industry (the smaller enterprises), the Keizai Doyu Kai ("Japan Committee for Economic Development"), the Nikkeiren ("Japan Federation of Employers' Associations"), and the Japan Foreign Trade Council, Inc. In publishing the guidelines, the *Keidanren Review* recognized that "along with the rapid advance of Japanese enterprises into overseas markets, many problems have cropped up in recipient countries, such as Thailand and Singapore." (It is interesting that what would soon prove to be the most explosive country, Indonesia, did not seem immediately to come to mind.) Adam Smith die-hards will raise eyebrows at that part of the preface to the code which admits that "the time-honored theories of economic liberalism are inadequate to meet the demands of the new times" but will be relieved that the "new approaches [will be] within the context of free enterprise and free competition."

Essentially the code calls for Japanese businessmen abroad to (1) assume a "basic posture [that will] ensure compatibility between the growth of the enterprise and the development of the host country; (2) promote "mutual trust [with] sound relations between labor and management . . . greater capital participation to local investors," and dissemination among the local population of "accurate information about their business operations"; (3) "employ and promote local employees [and] ensure their health and safety"; (4) see that "appropriate pre-assignment orientation and training" is given to personnel going abroad; (5) "promote transfer of technology" by training local employees on the job or in Japan; (6) contribute to the "international division of labor and the improvement of the balance of payments of the host country [by utilizing] to every extent possible the machinery, equipment and parts made in the host country, while extending technical guidance therefor"; (7) reinvest profits "in expansion and in the development of related industries" in the host country and take into account the host country's "international balance of payments position" when remitting profits; (8) "cooperate with the industries of the host country [and] thus prevent disturbance of the latter's economic order," and respect the host country's "distribution system"; and (9) cooperate with the host country in environmental conservation, education, and welfare by "harmonization with the local community [and] participation in the business and regional organizations of the host country."

When I visited Japan and Southeast Asia eighteen months after the adoption of the code, Japanese business activity was still under severe criticism for faults the code was intended to correct. Twenty-five months later, in July, 1975, the Thai cabinet was complaining of a trade imbalance caused by importation of luxury Japanese goods and was considering action against Japanese import restrictions and undercutting of Thai prices, as well as control and monopoly of exports.

Some serious steps have been taken to implement the preassignment training guideline. A fairly elaborate orientation program has been under way at the foot of Mount Fuji, conducted with expert Japanese and foreign lecturers.

To promote the code, several hundred companies organized the Japan Overseas Enterprises Association in 1974. The Association has been sending missions to host countries to study relevant subjects from local employment practices to local idiosyncracies and possible areas of conflict. It was preparing to open "country courses" for overseas personnel by mid-1975. In addition, according to Keidanren's senior managing director, Rikuzo Kotoh, the organization's Economic Cooperation Committee and its country committees (Japan-Thailand, Japan-Indonesia, etc.) "are trying to direct attention of top management to this important problem of getting along with local societies." Kotoh also stressed the role of the Export-Import Bank and the Ministry of International Trade and Industry (MITI) which are "in a position to advise" businessmen on the code.

In early 1975, MITI announced plans "to open consulting offices for Japanese businesses in six Southeast Asian countries" which, with a staff of Japanese officials, a senior local community leader, and two local young men, will "advise Japanese firms on social and cultural backgrounds and business practices."

The purely advisory role at home and abroad of government and business organizations in the enforcement of the nine points of the code underscores its congenital weakness. "The code of behavior is preventive in nature," Kotoh affirmed. "The important thing is that it is voluntary, its essence is voluntary restraint." He admitted that there might be a "need for legal sanctions to punish those who violate the code" but expressed the hope that "voluntary restraint will make legal sanctions unnecessary." MITI is reported to be preparing a bill "to require businesses to submit detailed investment programs which could later be altered to suit the countries involved," a procedure which would replace the current system in which investments "are approved almost automatically by the Bank of Japan." One might validly wonder if the bill will receive the same ritual treatment given the recently shelved proposal aimed at dismantling interlocking stock schemes for which Liberal Democratic members of the Diet are said to be wishing a quiet death.

Predictably, reaction to the code has been cautious if not skeptical or even outright cynical. Kien Theeravit thought it should be given a chance. "The Japanese are in a state of change, and the guidelines could provide them with guidance," he observed, adding that for some Japanese businessmen in Thailand "some points in the code seem to be too abstract, and we may have to wait a bit longer for it to be effective." Ob Vasuratana recalled that he had told MITI Minister Nakasone that he thought the code would be easy for the older Japanese to talk about, but it would be more difficult for the younger businessmen who have "hot tempers and a superiority complex." An outstanding Indonesian intellectual wondered if the code was concerned with cosmetics or fundamental change. Japanese Ambassador Fujizaki in Bangkok felt that "the special efforts to change the personal behavior of the Japanese will need decades rather than years to take effect; even today so many Japanese are not exposed to foreigners." S. B. Judono and Ali Noorluddin in Jakarta regretted that the code lacked sanctions and, as Noorluddin put it, "we would like to have a more effective control, but what can we do? It is strictly a Japanese thing." We shall examine some suggestions later about how the host Southeast Asian nations might control Japanese business activities.

Yusuf Panglaykim saw in the code a "starting point for a regional code of conduct," and Japanese Embassy Minister Komura did not think the lack of sanctions fatal. Accepting the "constructive tribalism" attributed to Japanese society and noting its manifestation in group travel led by flag-waving monitors, Komura asserted that "tribalism needs a flag, and there is no mode of enforcing the authority of the flag; so also the code is like a flag—there is no compulsion but only a moral force." Morihisa Emori, director of the Mitsubishi Research Institute, was less sanguine. He considered some parts of the code, such as that enjoining adjustment to local communities, "too idealistic [and they] can be interpreted in your own way and adjusted to business data." Governor Nagasu scoffed at the code's "etiquette theory," and the Keidanren's Kazuo Nukazawa categorically rejected the idea that a "code of behavior for overseas can solve any problems." He felt that the Japanese "have to change, we have to modify our education and we have to change our structure of society." He called for the drafting of "a code of behavior *within* Japan." Bernard Krisher summed up the skeptic's position: "You cannot legislate behavior."

Yet, the Japanese attempt at legislating behavior has apparently inspired other countries and even the United Nations to follow suit. In December, 1974, West German Chancellor Helmut Schmidt proposed a "code of good behavior" for multinationals doing business in his country and the United States and, later, for those operating in all of Europe. Earlier, in June, 1974, the United Nations Group of Eminent Persons investigating multinationals recommended the formulation of a "code of conduct," to be administered by a permanent commission, in hope that it would provide a legal basis for regulatory standards by individual governments. It is not yet clear what sanctions the United Nations might succeed in applying, and behavior by legislation is still very much a theory and a hope.

Political Change

But if behavior will not submit to legislation, particularly legislation without sanction, can the system that produces the behavior be overhauled by a new government under an opposition party voted in by the people? It should first be asked, can the opposition parties, the strongest of which is the Socialist, ever come to power in tradition-steeped Japan? Can Japanese society accept so much change?

We have seen how labor, although highly unionized, has submitted to the ritualism of the system, and it does not look like a promising base for political change. The Socialist party can never gain power so long as it relies on labor votes alone. However, Hiroharu Seki, noted political scientist at Tokyo University, pointed out that there has been a consistent 40 percent of Japanese voters who have been coming out in surveys as not supporting any party. "In the 1950s, most of these were not politically conscious," recalled Seki, "so they would vote for the Liberal Democrats." But the younger generation seems to have been registering opposition to the rigidity of the vertical system, Seki noted, and the no-support sector has been increasingly turning to one of the opposition parties. Furthermore, several important prefectures, including those embracing Tokyo and Yokohama and governing forty million people, are already in the hands of the opposition. Seki observed that the new local governors were "getting stronger, supported by citizen's movements, for instance, those against pollution." The Kanagawa prefecture was able to move effectively against the stationing of nuclear weapons on the U.S. naval base at Yokosuka.

Mitsubishi's Emori forsees "the possibility or probability that the left-wing parties may take over, since the conservatives have sat for too long a time, and it may be time for a change." Even before the oil crisis, it was predicted that the Liberal Democrats would soon lose their absolute majority. Surveys showed that if there had been a general election in the wake of Tanaka's resignation in late 1974, the Liberal Democrats would have received less than 40 percent of the vote; the Socialists, just under 30 percent; the Communists, 15 percent; the centrist Komeito, 12 percent; and the Democratic Socialists, 5 percent. But no such general election was found necessary when the Liberal Democrats came up with Takeo Miki as a compromise successor to Tanaka.

Miki is still in office, and no elections have been called. The resiliency of the vertical society, of which the Liberal Democrats are a functional part, has once more carried the day, overcoming the shocks of oil prices, Nixon Doctrine shifts, inflation, recession, and the Lockheed scandal.

But general elections are coming up in 1976, and the no-support floating vote may finally dislodge the Liberal Democrats from absolute majority. There would then be a choice of scenarios for a coalition government. Conceivably, the opposition parties could gang up on the Liberal Democrats. Such a coalition would be dominated by the Socialists (30 percent) and Communists (15 percent), and Japan would then in fact be governed by Marxists. The Establishment in Japan, says the *Economist*'s Norman Macrae, is not bothered at all by this prospect since a Marxist government, caught in the ritualism of the system, "will not know what on earth it wants." Seki admits that "even if the opposition parties win, changes in the social structure will not come right away." The conservative breastworks will not shatter easily. The coalition will attempt several assaults on it. The more reasonable demands will be accepted, e.g., pollution control. But if the government should "ask some things that would not be reasonable," then one Establishment member foresees that "neither the workers nor the rest of the industry would accept," and the government would fall.

A more likely coalition would be that of the Liberal Democrats, with perhaps 40 percent, and the Komeito, the "Clean Government" party based on a Buddhist sect, who would actually hold the balance with about 12 percent of the vote. One might throw in for a safety margin the non-Marxist Democratic Socialists (5 percent) who have managed to take what some have characterized as "innocuous" positions between the conservatives and the Marxists. Such a combination would not be a challenge to the system. The junior members would serve to give it a progressive face, but the dominant Liberal Democrats would see to it that no fundamental social change is provoked. Since it would not be a threat to the system, the system would support such a coalition, and it could last indefinitely.

X

Countervailing Power?

While awaiting the improbable day of domestic social change in Japan, the Southeast Asian nations must, urges one Indonesian technocrat, "develop economic and political countervailing power."

Indonesian technocrat Yusuf Panglaykim, one of those most awed by it, views the Japanese juggernaut as an extension of the Imperial Japanese Army. He is impressed by the finding in a study by Adams and Kobayashi[1] that 90 percent of the managers in Japanese business today were once officers of the imperial army generation of *Showa*. "Because of their discipline," Panglaykim said in Jakarta, "nobody can compete with them." He analyzes the problem as simply matching bigness with bigness and warned that "creating atomistic structures to compete with gigantic organizations simply will not work." He is so concerned with the reality of Japanese bigness that he fears that the Japanese will swallow "even the Americans, unless the U.S. antitrust laws are made more flexible." He would like to pit Indonesia, Inc., against Japan, Inc. He would like to see business develop "larger and more efficient units" and then combine with "government, bureaucracy, and technocrats [into an] Indonesian corporation capable of facing the Japanese-based multinational corporation." To do this, he sees the need for "developing the country's own institutions and mechanisms for bargaining."

Matching Japan's "big" institutions without matching the centuries of homogeneous cultural development that produced them may not be such an easy task. Far from being racially and culturally homogeneous, Indonesia today is still shaken with stubborn centrifugal cultural forces, and it is perhaps a tribute to the predom-

---

[1]T. F. M. Adams and N. Kobayashi, *The World of Japanese Business* (London: Ward Lock, Ltd., 1969), pp. 116-17.

inantly Javanese leadership in Jakarta that they have managed so far to keep the country together. In the east, the inhabitants of West Irian—over whom Sukarno successfully laid claim to sovereignty on the tenuous ground that they had also been Dutch subjects governed from Java, but who bear no cultural or racial affinity with the Javanese—are showing secessionist sentiments. In the west live the Achinese, whose kingdom once straddled most of Sumatra and parts of Malaysia and who are proud to have been the last nation in the archipelago to be subdued by the Dutch. They have never quite accepted the rule from Jakarta, which some of their more outspoken nationalists have characterized as "Javanese neocolonialism." In the northeast, the Maluccans are restless, thousands of them are in exile in Holland where they staged violent demonstrations in 1975. In the northwest, Marcos profits from Jakarta's moderating influence on the Muslim rebels. Indonesia is not happy over the prospect of a successful secession by Filipino Muslims for fear it could encourage secession within Indonesia itself.

"Big" institutions hurriedly erected on such a heterogeneous and brittle base would tend to be artificial and unstable. Pertamina, the only real Indonesian giant (which Panglaykim wishes could be developed into an even bigger trading firm "like Jardine Mathieson," the Asian-based British company) is now in serious trouble. The government oil conglomerate, run by Lieutenant General Ibnu Sutowo (who was dismissed in early 1976) has expanded into aviation, shipping, tourism, hotels, insurance, hospitals, general public works, steelmaking, and real estate. Hurrying to match the Japanese miracle of a government extending facilities and backing to private enterprise, Sutowo paradoxically did not wait for support from Indonesian government fiscal agencies but bypassed their restrictions on borrowings and went straight to the world market for short-term loans to finance his expansion. Performance did not come up to expectations, and $680 million was due in 1975 with no visible means of repayment. The Indonesian government had to appeal for outside help which came partly, and ironically, from the Japanese whose bigness Sutowo was striving somewhat flamboyantly to equal. In June, 1975, a group under the Bank of Tokyo came through with a $150 million loan and a U.S.-European consortium led by the Morgan Guaranty Trust Company with another of $425 million. In the wake of the crisis, Pertamina, by now dubbed the "prodigal state oil corporation" by the foreign press, was divested by the government of some of its holdings, principally the Krakatau steel plant in West Java. Some of the extravagant trappings of bigness also came under question, notably the Boeing 727 executive jet which Sutowo reportedly justified on the grounds that Pertamina's top men need to feel on an equal footing with rival oil tycoons.

The question was also being asked, said the *Washington Post*, "is Pertamina simply too big to use resources efficiently?" Perhaps *the* question to ask might be: Is bigness feasible in an unintegrated, developing heterogeneous society? The young Indonesian economist, Thee Kian-wie, who favors redirection of development goals, would answer, no. "It looks all right on paper," Thee said of Panglaykim's bigness theory, "if you subscribe to the acceleration-of-growth doctrine . . . but 'Indonesia, Inc.,' vs. 'Japan, Inc.,' will not really solve the problem." Puey Ungphakorn, the noted Thai intellectual, feels that, "except for enlarging the size of the market for our products, big-vs.-big should not be the approach even in ASEAN."

Dr. Sanoh Unakul, secretary-general of the Thai National Economic and Social Development Board, observed in an interview that Pertamina represents "bigness of the public enterprises." But, he added, "bigness can also come in terms of government policies and measures; by improving our economic policies and management, we would be able to provide a countervailing force to this Japanese drive." Sanoh admitted that "ASEAN can play a certain role" but warned that "we cannot rely completely on it as a countervailing power because the effort to build up this relationship constructively requires refinements of the existing procedures, which would be more than ASEAN can handle." He suggested that "it would be the job of each country to revise its rules."

These references to ASEAN reflect how Southeast Asian leaders rely on but at the same time doubt the efficacy of the eight-year-old regional alliance as a countervailing weight against the big powers, particularly neighboring Japan. Superior to its predecessors—the more or less anticommunist Association of Southeast Asia, which neutralist Sukarno refused to join, and the Maphilindo (Malaya, Indonesia, and the Philippines "bound together by ties of race and culture"), whose marked racial overtones made other Southeast Asian nations uneasy—ASEAN, encompassing a total population of 220 million, is being taken seriously in and out of the region. Some modest but real gains in pooled airlines services, highway projects, telecommunications, tourist promotion, and cultural exchange have been registered, and studies are under way for a joint supersonic airline and a shipping line. In Brussels, ASEAN has got the European Economic Community to create a joint study group to explore areas of economic cooperation which would include price stabilization for Southeast Asian exports.

Yet, there is reason to be less than optimistic about ASEAN's immediate future performance, given the deep racial, cultural, and religious animosities and suspicions that plague the region, in contrast with the cultural unity of Western Christendom which took many centuries and many wars to shape. Furthermore, the organization has inherited a raft of border disputes which continue to erode mutual confidence among the member states. There is a standing dispute between Thailand and Malaysia over the conversion to Buddhism of ethnic Malays in southern Thailand which is preventing joint action against insurgents in the border region. Some elements in Malaysia, led by the chief minister of Sabah, Tun Mustapha, are said to be supporting the Muslim rebellion in the southern Philippines.

Both issues underscore the reality that Southeast Asian national borders are mostly artificial, inherited from the accidents of European colonialism. The people of eastern Sabah and the Filipino Muslims in Sulu are of the same ethnic origins. There is speculation that official Malaysian ambivalence toward Mustapha's posture is its response to the pending Philippine claim to Sabah.[2] The claim has twice provoked diplomatic rupture between Malaysia and the Philippines. A plot to train Filipino Muslims to infiltrate Sabah, which was traced to Marcos and resulted in the massacre of the trainees when they balked at the last minute, has apparently not been forgotten.

In late 1974, Marcos, perhaps to provide himself with leverage with the Muslim rebels backed by Mustapha, revived the claim by formally proclaiming a member of the Kiram family as the Sultan of Sulu. It is the sultanate of Sulu's traditional inclusion of Sabah as part of its territory that is at the base of the Philippine claim. Predictably, Mustapha is backing another member of the Kiram family as heir to the throne, and what started out as former Philippine President Macapagal's grand and sympathetic response to Sukarno's ill-fated Konfrontasi has become a bargaining item in the settlement of the Muslim rebellion. In August, 1975, the impending resignation of Mustapha as chief minister of Sabah was announced in the press. This was closely followed by an announcement that his resignation would not involve his leaving as head of the state ruling party, the Berjaya-United Sabah National Organization. If Mustapha successfully clings to power, continuing tension between Malaysia and the Philippines may be expected. In early 1976, pro-Mustapha elements publicly accused Marcos of plotting Mustapha's assassination.

One weakening intraregional disagreement that is directly connected to relations with Japan is that over the Straits of Malacca, the narrow strip of water to which Malaysia, Singapore, and Indonesia are littoral states. The Straits have themselves been widely regarded as a regional countervailing force against Japan. It is Japan's oil lifeline to the Persian Gulf whence comes almost 90 percent of her requirements now totaling 280 million tons annually. The passage is also her coal, iron, and uranium route to western Australia. In 1973, 210 million tons of Persian Gulf oil in 1,700

---

[2] As a senator, I opposed the claim. I considered it legally defensible but politically inadvisable since it would inevitably run into, as it eventually did, the principle of self-determination. My fears, subsequently confirmed, were that the people of Sabah, pre-disposed by British-controlled newspapers to regard the Philippines as a wild American preserve, would not relish shifting their loyalty to Manila.

tankers and 40 million tons of Southeast Asian oil in 500 tankers passed through the Straits on its way to Japan.

Shortly before my visit to Jakarta in January, 1975, the 237,000-ton supertanker, *Showa Maru*, ran aground five miles off Singapore, causing massive oil spills. Malaysia claimed $10 million for operational costs and damage to marine life, while Indonesia claimed $51 million in operational costs and was preparing damage claims expected to reach $100 million. Singapore, which bore the brunt of the battle against the oil slicks, filed a modest $1.6 million for operational costs. In Jakarta, I heard officials make angry comments about the Japanese foreign minister's cavalier statement dismissing the affair as a matter purely between the shipping companies and the damage claimants. The Indonesian government came out with an eight-point declaration which reiterated a demand for a 200,000-ton limit in the Straits (the Japanese had been observing a self-imposed 250,000-ton ceiling, sending the heavier tankers through the Lombok Straits). Malaysia later lamented that "bordering the Straits is not so much a privilege as a burden"; that the livelihood of more than 100,000 Malaysians, dependent on fishing and providing 75 percent of the country's protein supply, was threatened; and that it would "take more than twenty-five years for the ecological cycle to resume again, if at all," after such a major oil spill.

Singapore's more cautious reaction reflected her deep differences with her littoral neighbors over the conduct of Straits traffic. "Singapore is not playing along with us," said Mohammad Sadli. "Her interest is in unrestricted freedom of passage, and of course we can understand her position." Protecting that position of major entrepot in Southeast Asia with shipping and bunkering facilities that thrive on unimpeded access, along with the attraction of foreign investments, is the major plank in Singapore's foreign policy, and it has required clever tightrope walking by Lee Kwan-yew. In 1974, Singapore's Port Authority handled 60 million tons of cargo, of which 45 million tons was bulk oil. The total handled the year before had been 61.3 million tons. The drop in volume, the first in its eleven years of operation, was traced largely to the oil crisis.

Singapore's lively, if judicious, defense of her position has led her to question the capability of Malaysia and Indonesia to carry out their assertion of control of the Straits. In November, 1973, for instance, American and Soviet naval vessels transited the passage without requesting permission from either of the asserting states. Indonesia has announced, however, that she will have the naval capacity to enforce her claims by 1979, having already acquired a destroyer from the United States.

If Indonesia should attempt to restrict passage of big-power naval units in the Straits, Singapore would stand to lose considerable port income. The U.S. Navy spends about $3 million annually for repairs, provisions, and fuel, and American sailors on shore leave contribute about $15 million to the economy. Soviet naval and merchant craft bring in more than $10 million each year.

In the meantime, Thailand has opposed the Philippine-Indonesian "archipelago" theory which holds that all waters between land in an island group belong to the country that owns the group. The theory would reduce the utility of Gulf of Siam ports where ships are serviced on the eastern sea route. Malaysia herself is reported to have her reservations since under the theory Indonesia's territorial waters would protrude between East and West Malaysia.

In March, 1975, a ministerial conference of the three littoral states decided on a traffic-separation scheme by which eastbound heavy-laden ships would be allotted the deepest channel and the lighter-laden westbound traffic would be given a shallower channel. The purely mechanical and provisional arrangement did not touch on the fundamental issues raised by the "archipelago" theory which keeps the littoral states basically disunited. Perhaps with this disunited front in mind, Indonesia, in spite of her apparently determined demands against Japan, is not really pressing for any final settlement of her differences with her colleagues that could turn the Straits into a potent ASEAN countervailing force. Sadli, in fact, believes that keeping the matter unsettled may make the straits a real Indonesian countervailing weapon. "If we ever settle the Malacca Straits issue in our favor," he told me, "we will be losing that leverage at the same time. As long as the question remains unsettled, we have leverage. The same is true with the Banda Sea. As soon as we say, 'No more fishing in the Banda Sea,' and the Japanese for some reason comply, we have lost some leverage."

No alternative to the straits route will make all the ASEAN states happy at the same time. The map at Table 17 illustrates how they would run. The Lombok route, more attractive than the Sunda route because it can accommodate ships up to 550,000 tons, was jointly surveyed by Japan and Indonesia in 1973 and found to be feasible although it would add 1,100 miles, two to three shipping days, and increase costs by about 8 percent. Japanese experts were to assist Indonesians in a more detailed survey beginning in May, 1975. Both the Sunda and Lombok routes would divert shipping from Singapore at a rate that could be disastrous to her port income, since about 80 percent of the shipping that passes through the Malacca Straits and is serviced at her port facilities is tankers bound for Japan. The diversion could also inflict worse damage on Gulf of Siam port business than the plans to limit Malacca traffic.

The idea of building a canal across the Kra Isthmus in southern Thailand fascinated the French and the British as early as the eighteenth century. In 1970, Thai industrialist K. Y. Chow commissioned a consulting firm to make feasibility studies which recommended a one-way, single-lane, west-to-east canal capable of taking 500,000-ton vessels. The recommendation was based on the finding that 95 percent of the traffic was west to east, the bulk of which was crude oil for Japan. There was also a projection on Japan's future oil needs, since updated because of the oil crisis and consequent interest in alternative sources of energy to 448 million tons by 1985, a 200-million-ton increase over the 1974 figure. A more modest, and less seriously considered, proposal by the Thai National Energy Authority calls for a canal that could handle vessels only up to 100,000 tons, which would not solve the problem posed by the Japanese supertankers.

A Kra canal would save 327 miles on the Japanese route and would save a total of over 1,800 miles when compared to the Lombok Straits route. "It would be a valuable link," Franklin Proud ob-

Table 17
Nautical Routes Between Persian Gulf and Japan

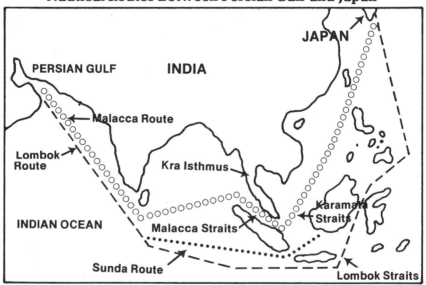

served in Bangkok, "to a world canal system which would include the Suez and the Panama." Canals have had a profound impact not only on the economies but also on the general outlook of nations. James Abegglen said in Tokyo that he subscribed to Herman Kahn's view that the Panama Canal made Brazil a Pacific country with a potential for competition for Japanese attention which should worry Southeast Asia.

The Chow proposal would create for Thailand a deep-water port that could service up to a million tons a year and a new complex for basic industries. Since the canal would be one-way, the crude oil carriers would return via the Malacca Straits and thus be serviced at Singapore. Proud noted that Lee Kwan-yew had supported the project.

With the political change in Thailand, interest in the canal diminished. The Japanese, from whom most of the financing had been expected, appeared to have lost interest, perhaps reassured by the disagreements between the littoral states on Malacca. The Japanese ambassador said categorically in Bangkok that "the Kra Canal project is dead." He added that there was "no keen interest" in Japan for an alternative project—a pipeline across the same isthmus—"because oil imports will not grow as it was expected."

But the *Showa Maru* grounding suddenly revived interest in the pipeline, which Marubeni Corporation had been promoting since 1971. It was reported after the grounding that the Japanese government had asked Marubeni to restudy the project as a possible venture by the Japanese government with private industries. At the same time, Thailand was also reported to have asked Kuwait and Saudi Arabia for assistance in financing the project. The plan is to lay 190 kilometers of pipeline, capable of carrying 100 million kiloliters of oil annually, and build refineries capable of producing 600,000 barrels a day and transshipping stations with storage capacity of 10 million kiloliters. The whole complex is estimated to cost $2.3 billion.

The intra-ASEAN competition over Japan's oil lifeline sharpened with Indonesia's announcement, simultaneous with the revival of interest in the Kra pipeline, that Pertamina was planning depots in the Semangka Gulf in south Sumatra where over ten million tons of crude oil could be stocked and then shipped to Japan in smaller tankers. In April, 1975, it was also announced that the Straits of Makassar, which are on the Lombok route, were now ready for supertankers of 200,000 tons or more.

Japan's show of interest in all the possible routes, none of which pleases all ASEAN countries at the same time, could be a clever *divide et impera* which causes a fairly deep chink in the ASEAN armor and reduces the effectiveness of cumulative ASEAN control of the passages as a countervailing force. Furthermore, China's upcoming capacity, as dramatized in Selig Harrison's recent findings, to produce oil in volumes paralleling those of the Persian Gulf could have a significant effect on ASEAN's trump cards, although it is not clear how much China would export.[3] Kazuo Nukazawa said in an interview in Tokyo that contrary to some impressions about the quality of Chinese oil (Mrs. Marcos had obtained some during her 1974 visit to Peking which was later reported to be unfit for Philippine refineries and was being considered for re-export), "Chinese oil is very good as far as sulfur content is concerned." (Its high wax content has turned out to be the real problem.) Although he foresaw pricing difficulties because of ideology ("the Chinese insist on labor costs as essential according to Marxist-Leninist economies"), Nukazawa confidently dismissed the Malacca-Lombok

[3]Selig S. Harrison, "Time Bomb in East Asia," *Foreign Policy* 20 (Fall 1975): 3-27.

dilemma: "We could rely more on Chinese oil or import from Siberia." (This is a confidence which may not be based on realistic projections of the oil export potential of both China and the Soviet Union.) In August, 1975, a visit to Caracas by Deputy Prime Minister Takeo Fukuda appeared to signal initial negotiations for a long-term agreement that could give Venezuela up to 10 percent of the Japanese crude oil market.

Japan continues to show interest in cooperation within ASPAC (Asian and Pacific Council) of which it is a member but which is now being phased out with the passing of the anticommunist fever in East and Southeast Asia (Taiwan is a founding member). One of ASPAC's creations, the Economic Operation Center or ECOCEN, with headquarters in Bangkok, is expected to be kept alive indefinitely by the member governments. ECOCEN's director, Dr. Vichitwong Na Phomphet, spoke warmly in an interview of Japanese government cooperation in joint studies on Japanese activities in Thailand in the fields of trading, labor, financing, and economic assistance. This cooperation could promote more understanding and cordiality between Japan and the Southeast Asian nations, but it is evident that neither ASPAC nor ECOCEN is of any use as a counterweight for Southeast Asia.

In the quest for more effective countervailing power, Indonesia has contemplated and tried the spreading of the foreign investment portfolio among as many of the developed countries as possible so that they might act as mutual counterweights. In the late 1960s, Sadli had advocated it as minister for investments and had traveled widely to promote interest among European and Arab countries. I asked him in January, 1975, if the plan had made progress. "It's not very effective," he admitted. "The U.S. is still number one in terms of dollars, the Japanese number one in terms of number of projects, a significant group is the overseas Chinese from Hong Kong, Singapore, and Taiwan, and then after that come the European investors." He noted, however, that "the flow from Europe is going on, and although it could not match the U.S. and the Japanese, a significant European presence, even in qualitative terms, may be enough of a countervailing force, an alternative for the Indonesian government to being solely dependent on Japanese know-how and investment." As to the Middle East, which can provide money but not technology or capital equipment, Sadli noted the ironic twist in the fact that the $200 million obtained in "a special deal between the Shah of Iran and President Suharto at World Bank terms [will all] be used in Japan." Japan's dominant position in technology and equipment supplies diminishes the effectiveness of Arab money as a countervailing force; Arab money, because of these purchases, may even enhance certain aspects of Southeast Asian dependence on Japan.

Southeast Asian nations like Indonesia may also be counting on an emerging Japanese-American economic rivalry for countervailing power. But as the *Far Eastern Economic Review* pointedly observed,

"The validity of the 'countervailing power' concept in the context of political-economical relationships dominated by multinational companies—which raise their money on the international money market, act in trans-national groupings and often do more to define than heed any nation's national interest—is doubtful."[4] In any case, mutual "counterweighting" becomes a myth in practice since, as Thee Kian-wie pointed out in Jakarta, "Japanese business is able to give domestic joint-venture partners a deal which looks better than any deal, European or American—the so-called package deal." We have seen how this irresistible deal has made "well-paid fronts" of Indonesian partners and provided the Japanese with control of policy, supplies, and marketing.

The control of waters, "bigness," counterweighting of foreign investors, regional cooperation—all these potential countervailing forces, even if perfected, would seem to screen from view what now appears to be the only hard reality, namely, the incompatibility between a growth-oriented development strategy which commits Southeast Asia to an ever-increasing and more irrevocable dependence on developed nations, principally Japan, and the avowed goal of basic development. The arduous and frustrating quest for countervailing power brings the searchers back to the question which they seem so assiduously to evade: Should current development goals be changed?

"This search for an alternative growth path," stressed Soedjatmoko in a 1973 speech at Sophia University, "is not simply a matter of ideological preference but—considerations of morality and equity aside—a political necessity for the survival of these nations." Like Mahbub ul Haq, Soedjatmoko suggests that Southeast Asians develop "a certain capacity for finding fulfillment and joy in their own cultural activities and a capacity to find meaning in their lives at what, for a long time, inevitably will have to be low levels of per capita income." Otherwise, he predicts that the region, like all poor countries unwilling to accept this reality, "will be doomed to be only consumers of the industrial and cultural products of the rich countries, prisoners of a bloated appetite for material things the country as a whole cannot afford."

How would Japan react to a radical shift in development strategy among Southeast Asian nations—a shift that would result in the dismantling of much of Japan's overseas investment and have a shattering impact on her domestic standard of living, her economics, her society, her politics? How would other powers, similarly affected but more militarily prepared, like the United States, meet the challenge?

The key to the answers to these questions may be found in the emerging world power picture.

---

[4]"Indonesia '74 Focus," *Far Eastern Economic Review* 86 (November 15, 1974): 5.

XI

The Crisis Potential and the Power Balance

When Japan entered World War II, it had a stockpile left of only one year's supply of oil. The crippling of the U.S. Navy at Pearl Harbor enabled the Japanese Navy to transport the invading armies in lightning thrusts southward to mineral-laden western colonies such as oil-rich Indonesia. We have seen how Japan's postwar economy now forces it ever more to depend on imports for oil and raw materials, in some cases for as much as 100 percent (see Table 13, page 53). Japan is not alone in this predicament. The magnitude of the problem of raw materials, not only for Japan but also for the entire community of developed nations, is underscored by the little-discussed projections of the United States' own dependence. The United States by the year 2000 will be 100 percent dependent on imports for such resources as manganese, aluminum, cobalt, tungsten, and tin and more than 50 percent for copper, iron, nickel, zinc, and sulfur.

The Boston Consulting Group breaks down its prediction of cumulative Japanese direct foreign investment of $28-$40 billion through 1980 (which, as has been seen, is more modest than Tokyo's own MITI forecast of $45 billion) as follows:

Resource development and materials processing	$13-20 billion
Manufacturing (nonprocessing)	$ 8-11 billion
Finance, commerce, and other	$ 7-9 billion

The Group stresses that "the range of resource development and materials processing investment reflects the difference between 5 and 15 percent compound growth through 1980," and will be important for expected growth in physical requirements during the period 1980-2000."[1]

In other words, Japan's hunger for raw materials will grow to proportions that will make the increase in import dependence even less reversible than it is today. Japan will be forced more and more to concentrate its investments on exploitation of the host countries' resources for consumption by industries at home. As has been seen, in 1975, 32 percent of Japan's approved overseas investment of $10 billion was directed to the five ASEAN nations. More than half of this ASEAN share, $810 million, went to Indonesia. (Thailand got $160 million.) The concentration on Indonesia reflects not only Indonesia's size but more importantly its abundance of resources, even excluding oil. Abegglen points out that his projections on resource development investment will be largely "in non-energy-related materials" (the United States is expected to continue to dominate oil exploration and production in Southeast Asia). Japanese investment in Indonesia is primarily resource oriented. Of the $405 million invested from June, 1967, to June, 1973, $126 million went to mineral, forestry, and fishing development. Another $211 million went to manufacturing which was mostly in textile mills which also produce semiprocessed raw materials for Japanese industry.

Were Indonesia by itself or in agreement with other ASEAN nations to decide on a regional redirection of development strategy that would substantially reduce the massive foreign exploitation of domestic natural resources, how would Japan, the United States, and other developed nations react? Can political leaders either in the democratic or in the communist developed nations bring themselves to lead their peoples toward a reduction of their own expectations and a changing of *their* life styles to adjust themselves to drastically diminished growth due to shortages of imported raw materials, cheap overseas labor, and opportunities for profitable foreign investment?

It is possible, says a study by the Overseas Development Council, that the people, at least in America, "may be well ahead of their leaders" in being prepared to make sacrifices for the poor of the world. The study cites a survey made by the Overseas Development Council in Chicago which showed that "nearly three out of every four Americans were willing to go without meat once a day and to cut out all unessential uses of fertilizer at home so that food and fertilizer could be shipped to countries abroad to combat food shortages."[2] But not eating meat once a day may be somewhat

---

[1]Boston Consulting Group, *Japan in 1980.*

[2]James W. Howe, and the staff of the Overseas Development Council, *The U.S. and World Development: Agenda for Action, 1975* (New York: Overseas Development Council, 1975), p. 70.

easier to bear than adjusting to lower overall rates of growth and simpler overall living patterns.

Furthermore, if the people are ahead of the leaders, the corporations appear to be ahead of the people. The overseas investment drive, spearheaded by the giant global enterprises, has begun to take on a sort of messianic sense of mission. Admiral Alfred Thayer Mahan's nineteenth-century Manifest Destiny once moved Assistant Secretary of the Navy Theodore Roosevelt to take advantage of the absence of the secretary to send Commodore Dewey to sink the Spanish flotilla in Manila Bay and put America on the road to empire. A recent study by the U.S. National War College's Strategic Research Group would entrust the global corporations with the very same mission with which Mahan and Roosevelt charged the U.S. Navy in 1898. The "osmotic action" of the multinational enterprise, "preponderantly American," says the study, "transmits and transfuses not only American methods of business operation, banking and marketing techniques; but our legal systems and concepts, our political philosophies, our ways of communicating and ideas of mobility, and a measure of the humanities and arts peculiar to our civilization." McKinley had similarly blessed Roosevelt's officious plunge into empire-building as a divinely sanctioned commission to "civilize and Christianize" the Filipinos who were 95 percent Roman Catholic and whose leaders in the then raging revolution against Spain had been educated in Manila universities older than Harvard. The Filipinos rejected this "civilizing" offer, and the United States responded by rechristening the Filipino revolutionary army as "insurrectos" and engaging them in a bloody three-year war of "pacification."

How will the United States react to a rejection of the new civilizing mission of her global enterprises? In the current mood of withdrawal from Asian conflict and given its worldwide range of options in markets and fields of investment, the reaction of the United States might well be "take us or leave us." But it is not easy to carry out a threat to pack up and walk away from billions of dollars of investment. The Japanese said as much to the Thais when the students protested pollution expected from planned Japanese petrochemical projects. But the Japanese are still in Thailand with an increasing volume and variety of investments, for the argument of geographic proximity is irrefutable, and breaking camp involves profound economic and social changes at home.

The Japanese are careful not to indulge in messianic or apocalyptic justifications in Southeast Asia for fear of reviving memories of the ill-fated Greater East Asia Co-Prosperity Sphere with which they had sought vainly to legitimate their belligerent *Nanshin* in the thirties and forties. Yet, it is they who need more diversionary self-justifying rhetoric, for their "bicycle-action" economy roots them in overseas investment more irrevocably than the United States and other developed nations. While, conceivably, the developed world might come up in this century with new sources of sufficient energy to replace oil, there are no significant signs of substitutes being found for the other raw materials which Japan is sorely lacking.

Recent studies such as that done in 1973 by John K. Emmerson and Leonard Humphreys (*Will Japan Rearm?*) for the American Enterprise Institute for Public Policy Research and the Hoover Institute on War, Revolution and Peace have shown that Japan's Self-Defense Forces (SDF) are far from being an instrument for the protection of its overseas trade and investment. By 1972, the SDF's strength had been fixed at 260,000 officers and men, outnumbered even by Indonesia's 317,000. Originally called the National Safety Force and established in 1952 as a 75,000-man army to defend Japan in view of the U.S. armed forces exodus to the Korean war, it has been declared in violation of the no-war clause of the Japanese constitution. As of mid-1975, an appeal to the higher courts by the Japanese government was still pending.

Per capita Japanese defense spending for 1971 was $18 compared to $378 for the United States in the same year. In 1975, the Japanese figure was expected to rise to $30 with a total SDF strength of 336,000 men and 66,000 reservists. Although Japan's present military posture is numerically modest and purely defensive, its potential for independent and self-sustained conversion to a conventional and nuclear power cannot be denied. By 1969, Japan was already manufacturing 97 percent of its own ammunition and 84 percent of its ordnance, aircraft, tanks, and naval craft. Japan was the fourth in the world to launch a space satellite (after the United States, the USSR, and France). Some experts say it could develop a guided missile with a nuclear warhead "within a year or two of a decision to go ahead." Other experts believe an India-type nuclear explosion could be produced in Japan within two to six months.[3]

Most Japanese I interviewed in Japan and Southeast Asia agreed that Japan would not rearm and would never "go to war over the Straits of Malacca." A few were not so sure. Kazuji Nagasu mentioned business leaders who have "raised the Malacca Straits doctrine—that the Straits were Japan's lifeline and had to be secure from foreign threat." The Malacca issue is symbolic of the total problem faced by Japan, as Nagasu put it, "in the years ahead when $30-40 billion of Japan's interests are vulnerable to [Southeast Asian] nationalism."

"How will the Japanese public, which is totally uninformed about Southeast Asia," Nagasu asked, "react if those interests

---

[3]Keyes Beech, "Japan, the Ultimate Domino?" *Saturday Review*, August 23, 1975, pp. 17 and 83.

appear to be threatened? Will the public demand that they be defended and that Japanese residents be rescued? Will the public panic at alarmist reports and clamor for dispatch of self-defense forces to 'save human lives'?" Nagasu then pointed out that "Japan now ranks seventh in military expenditures, the highest rate among all nonnuclear countries." (The SDF's expanded activities now include training officers from several Asian countries, including Indonesia and Thailand.)

Some U.S. observers do not take warnings like Nagasu's seriously. Keyes Beech, veteran correspondent in Asia, singles out Japan's utter dependence on raw materials, of which it "was sharply reminded" by the 1973 Arab oil squeeze, as the biggest deterrent to a major Japanese defense buildup. Furthermore, Beech asserts that "no amount of military power could guarantee the passage of Japanese tankers from the Persian Gulf through the Straits of Malacca." And, as has been seen, Singapore's taunt that neither Indonesia nor Malaysia can, without naval capacity, prevent passage in the Malacca Straits by big powers has been confirmed in several instances in which U.S. and Soviet naval units freely transited without consent of the littoral states. Yet, it was precisely this dependence that pushed Japan southward and into World War II. Beech does admit that "if Japan was threatened, the situation could well be different. But Japan does not feel threatened."[4]

Rising nationalism and consequent changes in development strategies in Southeast Asia could make Japan feel threatened. However, although Japan's industry could quickly be transformed to arms production, Japan's pacifist mood might take more time to change.

As I emerged from the Export-Import Bank in Tokyo in January, 1975, I saw a lone truck pass by decorated with the Japanese and Nationalist Chinese flags. It was empty save for one passenger who was obviously operating the public address system which was blaring forth a *senso no uta* ("war song") of the Imperial Japanese Army with which my ears had become all too familiar during the years of Japanese occupation of the Philippines. "It is a right-wing fringe group," explained my interpreter. "We let them go around playing songs and making speeches—nobody pays them attention."

But the "nonfringe" militaristic rightists are apparently taken more seriously than that lonely street haranguer. In 1971, there were 400 registered rightist organizations in the country with a total membership of 120,000, an increase of 60 percent over the 1960 figure. There were also some 3,500 so-called gangster groups with 140,000 members supporting right-wing causes, and 30 rightist student groups with a total of 300,000 members. The aggregate mass

---

[4]Beech, "Japan, the Ultimate Domino?"

support for these groups was estimated by rightist sources at more than 2.5 million, and their first goal is to eliminate the no-war clause in the constitution.

All of Japan's major political parties oppose remilitarization, but there is a vaguely identifiable right wing in the Liberal Democratic party, including former Prime Minister Nobusuke Kishi, which has consistently championed the elimination of the restrictive clause. Kishi has been reported to be chairman of a Dietmen's League for an Autonomous Constitution, claiming 264 of the total 741 Diet members. Yukio Mishima's ritual suicide in 1970 failed to arouse the SDF. Two years later an *Asahi* multiple-choice survey showed that 53 percent of the Japanese people preferred that their nation follow the course of "a welfare nation," 20 percent preferred a policy of "aid to developing nations and peaceful co-existence," 9 percent wanted Japan to become an "economic big power," and only 3 percent advocated "military big power" status. But an almost simultaneous survey by the *Tokyo Shimbun* showed that 30.3 percent believed Japanese militarism was reviving, 29.8 percent did not believe so, and 25.1 percent were undecided. The 1973 American Enterprise Institute study mentioned previously concludes that "the Japanese lack ambition for a military role." "But some," warns the study, "take a fatalistic attitude, not uncommon in their culture, that there are certain inevitable trends which it is hopeless to resist." Certain forces in and out of Japan may help to make those trends "inevitable."

The influential Keidanren has a Defense Production Committee whose chairman, then also the chairman of the board of Mitsubishi Heavy Industries, once made it clear that in spite of "relaxation of tension in Asia, Japan would still require a powerful defensive force." The director of Nikkeiren has also called for "a careful look at the defense problem in view of the need to secure energy sources abroad" and believes "constitutional revision necessary to national defense." These voices, combined with those of the other elements of the right, could influence trends from the inside. They could also be assisted by external forces.

The cold war of the seventies is mainly between China and the Soviet Union, and the Japanese appear to stand to profit from it in the short term, just as they did from its predecessor of the fifties. Both the Chinese and the Soviets are wooing Japan, and the first tempting gifts from both sides are those of oil. China appears to have an edge with its bargain-priced shipments which in 1975 were projected to reach twelve million tons. Contractual arrangements for Siberian oil and natural gas development seem for the moment bogged down.

The Chinese have warmed the cockles of the Japanese moderates' hearts with their support, first voiced by Chou En-lai in 1973, of the U.S.-Japan Security Treaty and even of the SDF. It appears to be China's calculation that the American shield will keep Japanese militarists without popular support and make closer Japanese ties with the Soviet Union unnecessary. All this could change when both Mao and Chou are gone if new Chinese leaders opt to return to the Soviet embrace for more effective counterbalancing against the United States. A less moderate Chinese leadership could thus help the cause of Japanese militarism by providing it with a potential enemy. Locating such an enemy is important for militarism. The Emmerson-Humphreys study has found that "without a hypothetical enemy the SDF cannot realistically gauge requirements or coordinate plans for defense [and that] naming China or the Soviet Union as an enemy, even though only for SDF planning purposes, could furnish propaganda opportunities to the left." The left could be stymied by a militant Sino-Soviet alliance.

Talk of Sino-Soviet rapprochement is, of course, purely speculative. In September, the Soviet Defense Ministry daily, *Red Star*, warned that "Peking's attempts to involve Japan in its anti-Soviet policy can harm the national interest of Japan and complicate its international relationships."

The delicate equilibrium which continues to give Japan reason not to rearm rests precariously on U.S. calculations. Northeast Asia is back in focus in U.S. policy after what Beech calls "a disastrous detour to Southeast Asia."[5] The talks in August, 1975, between U.S. Defense Secretary James Schlesinger and Japanese Defense Agency (JDA) Director-General Michita Sakata centered on the Korean peninsula within the framework of "defense concept-sharing." Schlesinger publicly chided the Japanese for being "too passive" in matters of defense. He appeared to be rubbing in charges of Japanese "free riding." The parties agreed to set up a "consultative organ" to be inaugurated in early 1976. Meanwhile, *Asahi* listed "the intentions of the U.S. side as expectations on Japan" as including "(1) the securing of sea lanes, (2) the securing of anti-submarine capability, and (3) air defense duties." All of these objectives would mean "incorporation of the SDF in the U.S. Force's overall strategy concept."

The first two objectives could require the expansion of Japanese naval forces which in 1975 were expected to stand at 40,204 men in five regional units, with four to five escort flotillas, 250-280,000 tons, and a budget of $3.7 billion. Just how much expansion might be required would depend on interpretation, particularly of the objective of "securing of sea lanes." The *Nihon Keizai* spelled this out just before the Schlesinger visit as "the power to protect maritime shipping lanes [supply routes]." Just how far this "power" is supposed to stretch has not yet been made clear. But

---

[5]Beech, "Japan, the Ultimate Domino?"

Japan's supply routes reach all the way to the Persian Gulf and pass through the Straits of Malacca. If this is the vision of U.S.-Japanese "defense concept-sharing," then it confirms the fears of pacifists like Nagasu and the ambitions of industrialists like the Nikkeiren director who, as we have seen, could not divorce the defense problem from the question of "energy sources abroad." Thus, U.S. policy would seem to be firmly pushing the Japanese to develop a capacity for a military and naval response to such unfavorable nationalistic policies abroad as would imperil their supply routes, their energy sources, or their investments.

U.S. congressional leaders apparently foresee this development and would like to head it off. On August 13, 1975, just two weeks before the Schlesinger visit, a U.S. congressional mission headed by Representative Lester Wolff, chairman of the House Foreign Affairs Subcommittee on Foreign Policy Research, arrived in Tokyo. In a press interview, Wolff stressed that because of restrictions in the Japanese constitution, "the SDF can be used only for purely self-defense purposes [and that it] cannot fully fulfill the role which the United States has hitherto demanded repeatedly of Japan." Wolff suggested instead "cooperation" in which Japan would "offer support in the economic and political fields" while the United States would give "support in the military field." Wolff became concerned over Japanese military resurgence in 1970 when he and his cochairman of a study mission, Representative J. Herbert Burke, reported to the House Foreign Affairs Committee that there seemed to be "a readiness to commit a substantial portion of Japan's vast wealth to the establishment of a major international military force." They said this would involve "increased spending, a much greater definition of her area of defense, nuclear capability, and a clear determination to be a military power on a scale not contemplated since World War II."

The U.S. Department of Defense apparently chose to ignore these congressional warnings to the seeming delight of Japanese industry. Made aware in advance of the agenda of the Schlesinger visit, Keidanren Defense Production Committee leaders, including Kawasaki Heavy Industries President Kiyoshi Yotsumoto and Mitsubishi Heavy Industries President Gakuji Moriya, called on JDA Director General Sakata three days before Schlesinger's arrival to make sure that the additional PXL (antisubmarine patrol) planes that would be required in implementing the Schlesinger proposals would be produced domestically instead of being imported from the United States. The production will involve Y500-600 billion (up to $2.2 billion). The planes would be deployed in 1982 by the Maritime Self-Defense Forces (MSDF). Just how much defense spending means to Japanese industry can be gleaned from the Keidanren's warning that "unless the PXL is manufactured at home, the aircraft industry will fall into a critical state."

The Soviet Union can be safely predicted to be unhappy if these SDF expansion plans are carried out. China's reaction is not easy to foretell. Assuming that China's overriding foreign and defense policy concern today is over encirclement by the Soviets, including Soviet penetration of the Indian Ocean, the Chinese leaders could decide that one more navy patrolling its surrounding waters and held under leash by the United States might just provide it with safety in numbers. Toleration of a Japanese naval buildup could deepen doubts already existing in the Third and Fourth Worlds about China's claim to leadership of world revolution, especially if the new Japanese military power is used to dissuade developing nations from adopting more independent and nationalistic economic policies.

The considerations that could lead Japan to "go nuclear" are somewhat different from those which would justify preparations for conventional warfare. Experts agree that Japan could opt for nuclear armament either (1) for prestige (e.g., to bully its way into the U.N. Security Council), or (2) because of loss of credibility in the U.S. nuclear deterrent, or (3) because of an increased perception of nuclear threat, possibly from China or the Soviet Union. But Japanese defense analysts think the idea preposterous since a nuclear power requires a "second-strike capability [and] after the first strike there wouldn't be anything left of Japan."

Whether Japan goes nuclear or not will not affect its potential in the use of conventional arms. And in the last two decades, many bloody conventional wars have, indeed, been fought in the shadow of the nuclear stalemate. At the moment, the Japanese people do not seem to be ready to support war. A *Tokyo Shimbun* survey in the Tokyo area in August, 1975, showed that, in case of war, 43.4 percent would resist fighting, 14.3 percent would not do anything, 12.3 percent would fight reluctantly, and only 5.7 percent would fight positively. A significant 20.7 percent, however, were undecided. Furthermore, the survey did not distinguish between a war among big powers (which is what the respondents, with Korea in mind, may have thought to be the issue) and a limited war or "protective action" to defend Japan's supply routes, access to raw materials, and foreign investments. Nor was there a survey on the use of armed power, short of actual war, to threaten or intimidate prospective defiers of Japan's interests among the developing nations, particularly those in Southeast Asia. Falling living standards, high unemployment, and frustrated expectations resulting from such defiance could bring about dramatic changes in Japanese views on rearmament.

If force, or the show of force, is not available for domestic or international reasons, Japan will have to resort to other means to maintain its overseas trade and investment position and its supply routes, which may not be controllable domestically or internationally. One such obvious means is intensified corruption. As has been seen, the tight cooperation between Japanese government and business has so far prevented U.S.-style legislative exposés which could permit quantifying of corrupt Japanese practices in overseas investments. Massive U.S. corruption abroad (Lockheed alone has been found to have doled out $25-30 million in foreign bribes in five years) has found a justification in the need to sustain the pace of U.S. foreign investment which in 1975 was estimated to generate 15 percent of the gross national product, 30 percent of the total profits of American corporations, and an estimated ten million American jobs. As has been seen, sales of the Japanese Big Six alone (see Table 13, page 53), most of it abroad, constituted 20 percent of the Japanese GNP in 1973. Given the more urgent pressures in the Japanese economy and the admitted, though not quantified, corruptive quality of Japanese overseas business activity, one may safely presume that at this point corruption by Japanese surpasses that by Americans in volume relative to gross investment.

More crucial than volume is the demoralizing impact that corruption can deliver to a developing society. It weakens the national will and heightens tensions. In democratic Thailand, the newly reopened safety valves of free expression might provide release for these tensions and bring about dialogue for a national consensus on peaceful change. In Indonesia, where these valves remain shut, the prospect will have to be accepted that the presence of Japan, as well as that of the United States, the Western Europeans, and the overseas Chinese, could continue to provoke not only petty "scapegoating" but also disturbances of a magnitude that could create internal vacuums of power which could suck the big nations into a messy and gory scramble.

Japan's dynamism and vulnerability are a rare and explosive combination. In 1941, they took Japan into World War II. Today, they constitute the crisis potential in Southeast Asia.

XII

Towards a New Ideology

In October, 1975, a strong delegation from Indonesia visited the United States for talks on economic and military aid. It was headed by Mohammad Sadli, Lieutenant General Ali Moertopo, firmly rehabilitated after the January, 1974, riots as deputy chief of BAKIN, and Daoed Joesoef, chairman of the board of directors of the Center for Strategic and International Studies which was founded by Moertopo. It was evident from their statements that there is to be no radical shift in Indonesia's development strategy. Foreign investment is to receive continued encouragement. The reality is that most foreign ventures will continue to be capital intensive, and the problem of employment creation is to be solved by government spending on infrastructure and public projects with the revenue expected from the foreign ventures.

While the continuation of the present trickle-down strategy will not trigger any quick retaliation that could involve the violence of arms or the equally explosive violence of massive corruption, we have seen that the character of this strategy is such that it could lead in the long run to precisely this kind of violence. For the more the volume of Japanese economic involvement increases in Southeast Asia, the larger and more complex looms the problem of the Japanese paradox—power and vulnerability—a combination which has been shown to be particularly flammable.

Meanwhile, there is time to search for formulas that might at least postpone what appears to be the inevitable explosion or perhaps, given a felicitous rearrangement in the power picture, prevent its detonation altogether.

The unique configuration of Japanese society makes the current debate on global corporations only partially relevant to the problem of Japanese penetration of developing countries, but it is an important relevance nonetheless. In 1973, the United Nations Department of Economic and Social Affairs prepared a working report to facilitate the deliberations of the Group of Eminent Persons, which the Economic and Social Council (ECOSOC), in 1972, had requested the United Nations Secretary-General to convene to "study the role of multinational corporations and their impact on the process of development, [to] prepare conclusions which may possibly be used by governments, [and to] submit recommendations for appropriate international action."

The working report recommended consideration of a "common code of behavior," a term and concept already enjoying wide currency among the Japanese. The code would place first stress on multinational labor union programs. It also called for home-country, host-country, regional, and international programs. On the host- and home-country level, the report rallied to the Calvo doctrine, now incorporated in the laws of several Latin American countries, that "foreign firms which appeal to their home governments in cases of dispute will be penalized accordingly" by the host country. It supported regional groupings that increase the bargaining power of developing nations "as has been demonstrated by the Andean group." It suggested that ECOSOC be made an international forum and the United Nations Secretariat an information-collecting center for problems on multinational corporations. It proposed a codification of all codes of behavior, a GATT (General Agreement on Tariffs and Trade)-type International trade Organization for international investment, the registration of multinationals with the United Nations, an international agreement on multinationals patterned after the existing Satellite Communications Agreement and the proposed European Company Law. The report finally recognized the lack of an international sanctioning authority and urged interim "voluntary conciliation or arbitration procedures."

Some of the Group of Eminent Persons were dissatisfied with the Secretariat's report since, as one of them put it, "it does not raise the question of alternatives and counterstrategies but seeks merely to reconcile conflicts within a system of continued expansion of multinational corporations."

After hearings held in late 1973, the Group released a report in the fall of 1974 entitled, "The Impact of Multinational Corporations on the Development Process and on International Relations," following which ECOSOC established an intergovernmental Commission on Transnational Corporations entrusted with developing recommendations for a code of conduct and overseeing the protection of host developing countries.

Although the Group's report appeared to accept the principle of conciliation, the major developed nations seemed to reject an implication in the report that there is fundamentally a hostile confrontation between multinationals and host developing countries. At the Commission's first session in March, 1975, France, West Germany, Italy, the United Kingdom, and the United States submitted a joint note on their "areas of concern" which included expropriation, international arbitration, and the question of stable investment climates. It is perhaps typical of Japan's low diplomatic profile that it did not join in the submission of the note. Secretary of State Henry Kissinger reflected the conciliation approach when he advocated in a Houston address in 1975 the creation of "intergovernmental systems" to resolve investment disputes on the basis of a "declaration of principles." One dissenting view is that of the Latin American countries who subscribe to the Charter of Economic Rights and Duties of States, which takes the position that not intergovernmental bodies but each state should be strengthened in the right to regulate multinationals and to prevent intervention by the latter in the internal affairs of a state.

The Latin American countries have drawn up their own set of ten principles (ASEAN countries have yet to agree on their own common code), some of which would be particularly difficult for Japanese to observe. For instance, one principle reads, "Multinationals shall not serve as an instrument of external policy of another state." As has been seen, not only is the Japanese trading company inextricably linked with state policy, but it is often difficult to determine which one is using the other.

The Commission in its first session recommended that the Information and Research Center on Transnational Corporations, established by ECOSOC in August, 1974, concentrate on researching those recommendations of the Group's report that would lead to the drafting of a code of conduct and the protection of host developing countries which are both essentially objectives of conciliation. There appeared to be only one proposal "by a number of representatives to study, as alternatives to the transnational corporations, other methods of internationalizing the production of goods and services and management." Although the report does not specify which countries had made the proposal, the fact that they suggested the Council for Mutual Economic Assistance (the Eastern European counterpart of the Organization for Economic Cooperation and Development) as a model would indicate that they were representatives from the communist bloc.

It would seem that neither the report of the Commission on Transnational Corporations, the ten Latin American guidelines, nor the minority alternative of the Eastern European countries comes squarely to grips with the long-term realities of the issue. The global enterprises are here to stay, and any attempt to destroy them or severely limit their activities could, as has been shown, be met with violent military or corruptive action. In the case of the Japanese, the dimension of sheer survival renders the issue even more acute. As has been shown, the decisive thrust of Japanese, as well as U.S. and European, investment is profit and is in large measure anti-developmental in the host countries since it introduces an artificial consumption ethic not rooted in the culture, traditions, or genuine needs of the population. It is also designed to make captive the sources of raw materials in the developing countries.

Furthermore, there is an evident unreadiness on the part of the developing nations to overhaul their development strategies in order to reduce drastically their dependence on foreign enterprises. Except in the left-wing totalitarian countries, there is no political will to force the population to accept the painful transition that such an overhauling would require. And the alternative of a left-wing dictatorship, which kills private initiative and imperils human rights, is an equally bleak prospect for the millions in the poorer nations.

The search for an alternative need not lead inexorably to the dead end of totalitarianism. The controversial Catholic churchman, Ivan Illich, questions not democracy but the distortions of capitalism when he complains that "each car which Brazil puts on the road denies fifty people good transportation by bus, each merchandised refrigerator reduces the chances of building a community freezer." Illich is not an economist and may not realize he is arguing for the "intermediary technology" which an increasing number of economists are suggesting for the maximization of employment in the process of industrialization. Australian political scientist Herbert Feith laments the suppression of dissent, the harassment of suspected minorities, and the use of forced labor in China. But he is not blind to the virtues of China's intermediary labor-intensive industries scattered in the rural areas with the peasants as the main beneficiaries of the wealth produced. Mahbub ul Haq told me that he shares this appreciation of China's innovativeness even as he also rejects repression of dissent. The impression that the search for an intermediary nonexploitative technology is confined to the Marxists is, of course, incorrect. In October, 1975, British economist E. L. Schumacher, the former head of Britain's National Coal Board, told a Texas audience of businessmen to "move back to smallness." Dr. Schumacher, author of the book, *Small Is Beautiful,* is now head of the London-based Intermediate Technology Development Group, established in 1965 "to provide this type of technology for the developing countries." He argued that "the small-scale enterprise could provide a solution to the problems faced by both rich and poor countries—excessive industrialization and the decline of rural areas, the massive energy demands of high-technology industry, the overwhelming capital investment required to sustain such industry and increasing unemployment."

What is not clear is whether Schumacher's research group will come up with proposals that will permit the multinationals to convert to small-scale technology without serious impairment of profits. And assuming that the proposals are there, it is not clear how the multinationals can be made to go through the inconvenience or perhaps even trauma of conversion. The *New York Times* reported that the chairman of the Koppers Company, responding to Schumacher, admitted the problem created by bigness but conceded that "voluntarism" was not enough to move businessmen to make the changes.

What might be needed is to move the study of the problem from the private to the public and international domain. The United Nations Commission on Transnational Corporations could retain its objective of conciliation, but it might redefine that objective. The present terms of the Commission's injunctions seem to be directed toward the conciliation of the development strategies of the host countries with the global-profit strategies of the world enterprises through the mutual acceptance of concessions, sometimes cosmetic in character, which do not strike at the heart of the question. Conciliation would be valid here if it were to seek to reduce the technological, financing, and distributive methods of global companies to dimensions within the reach of the host countries and not disruptive of their traditions.

The United Nations General Assembly resolution on "Development and International Economic Cooperation," adopted in its Seventh Special Session (September, 1975), calls on developed countries to assist developing countries "in the creation of suitable indigenous technology." It is an important and timely injunction and a recognition long overdue of the dubious effect of large-scale technology on developing economies. However, the General Assembly, perhaps awaiting recommendations to reach it from the Commission on Transnational Corporations, has yet to deal with the heart of the question. Enjoining governments without acknowledging the decisive role of the transnationals in the conversion of developing economies to "suitable indigenous technology" leaves the resolution somewhat hollow.

Any serious attempt to make this conversion possible should immediately concern itself with studies on how to reduce predictable resistance on the part of the transnationals. It should also consider how the conversion may be effected in developing countries without provoking those domestic convulsions that result in the suppression of human rights. One of the most crucial of these decisions was adopting the Universal Declaration of Human Rights. As has been seen, suppression of these rights and the shutting of the safety valves of free expression usually serve to aggravate the explosive impact of the transnationals on developing economies.

Specifically, the Information and Research Center could be asked by the Commission to:

1. Collate all available information on intermediate technology from member countries;

2. Study their applicability to various developing regions;

3. Study ways in which the superior organization and technology of the transnational corporations may be utilized to assist the developing nations in adopting this technology, if possible without serious impairment of profit for the corporations;

4. Study means for adopting this technology without violation of the provisions of the Universal Declaration of Human Rights;

5. Report its findings to ECOSOC.

ECOSOC could then draft a resolution for adoption by the General Assembly, based on the report, in which all the agencies of the United Nations would be enjoined to adopt it as part of their policy.

The device of conciliation by a shift in technology cannot solve all the problems attendant upon the awesome dimensions of the transnationals. One of these is their ability to manipulate prices and skirt tax laws by selling to their own affiliates or passing off gains or losses to these affiliates in a propitious fiscal year. But creating more receptiveness in the host developing countries by meeting their genuine technological needs might also produce more business volume for the transnationals that will maintain if not increase their level of profits. Even intermediate technology will require machinery and equipment which the host country may have to continue to import for a long time even after conversion. The multiplication of production units could even increase profits for the developed nations and help them to dissuade their transnationals from these manipulative practices. Furthermore, the robust development induced by the new technology could more quickly give the developing nations the strength with which to bargain with the big companies.

An innovative proposal within the framework of democracy and private enterprise is that proposed by Louis Kelso,[1] who advocates the restructuring of national credit systems to facilitate capital formation based on diffused ownership. Kelso's proposals, once ridiculed by traditional economists, have at last acquired respectability and are being successfully tested in the United States and abroad. The United Nations Commission should be asked to investi-

---

[1] *The Capitalist Manifesto* (New York: Random House, 1958). The 1976 annual report of the Joint Economic Commission of the U.S. Senate and House of Representatives recommends adoption of a national policy to foster the goal of broadened capital ownership. Among the theories proposed for adoption is the ESOP (Employee Stock Ownership Plans) advocated by Kelso. Four U.S. Federal statutes have already been passed encouraging this plan.

gate the relevance of these proposals to developing nations for whom Kelso offers the prospect of eventual liberation from reliance on foreign investment.

A massive conversion either to Kelso or to "smallness" would prosper better if there were ideological changes in the developed nations. George C. Lodge, author and professor at Harvard Business School, believes an ideological transformation may already be under way in America. The individualism of John Locke and Adam Smith is in the process of being augmented and replaced by communitarianism with its superior concern for justice and fairness.[2] Eventually, this concern might be extended to those beyond the bonds of American society but within the sphere of activity of American institutions like transnational corporations. Combined with the forces concerned with global redistribution and ecology, it could bring the nation and its economic institutions to accept growth that is tempered with justice.

The prospects for ideological transformation in Japan do not seem to be as promising. Japan is a much more closed society, and the vertical *ie* structure is not shaken easily by domestic or external tremors. But the system has also convincingly demonstrated its resiliency in the face of a series of economic and diplomatic *shokku*. If it responds to ideological change with the traditional "very difficult," it might also be willing to venture a reluctant but pragmatic "yes" to strategic deviations for its own protection.

It is in this spirit that Japan might now be approached and asked not to wait for grand shifts in the global strategy of developed nations but to take the initiative and respond with the innovative genius of the vertical *ie* to the challenge of technological conversion. What is at stake is its survival, and there seems to be no other long-term recourse unless Japan is to abandon its repudiation of militarism or continue in the combustible ways of corruption in order to defend its vulnerable economy. If it takes the pragmatic option, the Tokyo Express could be kept on the rails but on a new course with no serious collision in sight.

---

[2]George C. Lodge, *The New American Ideology* (New York: Knopf, 1975), pp. 17 and 179.

Selected Bibliography

In preparing this study I interviewed approximately one hundred people in Japan, Indonesia, Thailand, Hong Kong, Hawaii and mainland United States. With few exceptions, the interviews were tape-recorded and for the record. Among those interviewed were government officials and politicians as well as university professors, labor leaders, students, journalists, anthropologists, business leaders, bankers, diplomats and other private individuals.

I acknowledge with deep gratitude the assistance of the following institutions in arranging for these interviews: the International House of Japan, the Centre for Strategic and International Studies in Jakarta, the National Economic and Scientific Development Board in Bangkok, the Australian Institute of International Affairs, and the Political Science Department of the University of Hawaii. Although the interviews were not limited to those arranged by these organizations, I could not have reached the variety of knowledgeable interviewees that I feel I did reach without their generous cooperation.

The following books, articles and publications of various types were useful in the study and should prove useful as references.

Adams, T. F. M. and N. Kobayashi. *The World of Japanese Business.* London: Ward Lock, Ltd., 1969.

Alonza, Encarnacion. *Galicano Apacible, Portrait of a Filipino Patriot.* Manila, 1971.

Barnet, Richard J. and Ronald E. Müller. *Global Reach.* New York: Simon and Schuster, 1974.

Beech, Keyes. "Japan, the Ultimate Domino?" *Saturday Review,* August 23, 1975, pp. 15-19.

Boston Consulting Group. *Japan in 1980.* London: Financial Times, Ltd., 1974.

Centre for Strategic and International Studies. *Japanese-Indonesian Relations in the Seventies.* Jakarta: Papers presented at the First Japanese-Indonesian Conference (December 6-9, 1973), 1974.

Crouch, Harold. "The '15th January Affair' in Indonesia." *Dyason House Papers.* Melbourne: Australian Institute of International Affairs, August, 1974, pp. 1-5.

Emmerson, John K. and Leonard Humphreys. *Will Japan Rearm?* Washington, D.C.: American Enterprise Institute for Public Policy Research and the Hoover Institution on War, Revolution, and Peace (Stanford, California), 1973.

Gibney, Frank. *Japan, the Fragile Superpower.* New York: W. W. Norton, 1975.

Gwirtzman, Milton S. "Is Bribery Defensible?" *New York Times Magazine,* October 5, 1975, p. 19.

Halliday, Jon and Gavan McCormack. *Japanese Imperialism Today.* London: Pelican, 1973.

Harrison, Selig S. "Japan, Inc., Tempering Its Asian Goals." *Washington Post,* February 25, 1973.

_____. "Time Bomb in East Asia." *Foreign Policy* 20 (Fall 1975): 3-27.

Heller, Robert and Emily. *The Economic and Social Impact of Foreign Investment in Hawaii.* Honolulu: University of Hawaii Economic Research Center, 1973.

Howe, James W. and the staff of the Overseas Development Council. *The U.S. and World Development: Agenda for Action, 1975.* New York: Overseas Development Council, 1975.

"Indonesia '74 Focus." *Far Eastern Economic Review* 86 (November 15, 1974).

Kahn, Herman. *The Emerging Japanese Superstate.* Englewood Cliffs, New Jersey: Prentice-Hall, 1970.

Karnow, Stanley. "The Ardent Asian Suitors." *Saturday Review,* August 23, 1975, p. 28.

Keiji, Kobayashi. "An Asian Image of Japan." *Japan Interpreter* 7 (Spring 1971):

Komiya, Ryutaro. "Economy Planning in Japan." *Challenge* 18 (May/June 1975): 9-20.

Kunihiro, Masao. "Indigenous Barriers to Communication." *The Wheel Extended* (Toyota Quarterly Review) 3 (Spring 1974): 11-17.

Lockwood, William. *The Economic Development of Japan.* Princeton, New Jersey: Princeton University Press, 1968.

Lodge, George C. *The New American Ideology.* New York: Knopf, 1975.

Macrae, Norman. "Pacific Century, 1975-2075?" *Economist* 254 (January 4, 1975): 15-35.

Nagasu, Kazuji. "The Super-Illusions of an Economic Superpower." *Japan Interpreter*, Summer/Autumn, 1974, pp. 149-64.

Nakane, Chie. *Japanese Society*. London: Penguin, 1973.

_____. "Social Background of Japanese in Southeast Asia." *The Developing Economies* 10 (June 1972): 115-25.

_____. "Strangers Within the Gate." *Insight*, January 24, 1973, pp. 19-22.

Nomura Research Institute. *Multinationalization of Japanese Companies*. Tokyo: Nomura Research Report, June 25, 1973.

Panglaykim, Yusuf. *Business Relations Between Indonesia and Japan*. Jakarta: Centre for Strategic and International Studies, 1974.

Servan-Schreiber, J. J. *The American Challenge*. New York: Avon, 1969.

Simon, Sheldon W. *Asian Neutralism and U.S. Policy*. Washington, D.C.: American Enterprise Institute for Public Policy Research, 1975.

Theeravit, Kien. *The Japanese-Thai Economic Interaction as of October 1973*. Bangkok: Chulalongkorn University, 1974.

United Nations, Department of Economic and Social Affairs. *Multinational Corporations in World Development*. New York: United Nations, 1973.

United Nations, Economic and Social Council. *Commission on Transnational Corporations: Report on the First Session* (17-28 March 1975) Supplement 12. New York, 1975, pp. 20-22.

United Nations. *Summary of the Hearings Before the Group of Eminent Persons to Study the Impact of Multinational Corporations on Development and on International Relations*. New York, 1974.

Weinstein, Franklin B. "The Indonesian Elite's View of the World and the Foreign Policy of Development." *Indonesia*, October, 1971, pp. 97-131.

_____. "The Uses of Foreign Policy in Indonesia." Unpublished Cornell University doctoral thesis, 1972.

_____. "World Politics and World Powers: The View from Djakarta." *Asia* 27 (Autumn 1972): 37-61.

Wionczek, Miguel S. "Rules for Multinationals: The Latin American Context." *Worldview*, October, 1975, pp. 27-34.

Wroniak, Alexander. "Technological Transfer in Eastern Europe: Receiving Countries." *East-West Trade and the Technology Gap*, ed. Stanislaw Wasowski. New York: Praeger, 1970.

Yano, Toru. "Postwar Structure of 'Nanshin'." *Japan Echo* 1 (1974).

Appendix

Selections from
The Japanese-Thai Economic Interaction (as of October 1973)
by Chulalongkorn University Professor Dr. Kien Theeravit,
Bangkok, Thailand.*

Abstract

This is a study of contemporary Japanese-Thai economic relations with special emphasis on Japanese economic activities in Thailand. As an introduction to the subject, an attempt is made to compare the present economic structures of Japan and Thailand. Japan is shown to be an industrial nation whereas Thailand is an agricultural society. The difference in the levels of economic development of the two countries creates conditions favorable to economic interaction. It encourages commerce between the two countries as well as a trend toward complementarity of economic activity. The Japanese model of economic development is also attractive to many Thai economic planners. As the government of Meiji Japan, the Thai government has taken the lead in economic development by building national economic infrastructure.

At present, however, the economic systems of the two countries have generated different patterns of organization. The Japanese are organizationally strong in both the agricultural and the industrial sectors whereas the Thais are dismally weak. The expansions of the well-organized Japanese big businesses (*Keiretsu*) into Thailand have presented both an opportunity and a threat to Thailand's junior entrepreneurs. The latter are forced by the veteran economic intruders to accept a topdog-underdog pattern of economic relationship or face unfavorable economic consequences. The organizationally strong Japanese businessmen are also advantaged over their Thai counterparts in their business dealing: the former can

---

*Translated from Thai into English by Kien Theeravit.

systematically translate their interests into their national policy in a way which cannot be done in Thailand. The Thais lack not only organized interest groups to articulate their demands, but also a stabilised parliamentary system and representative government.

There is also a "sophistication gap" between Japan and Thailand in the commercial and service sectors of their economies. The so-called *shoji* (general trading companies) have no comparable counterpart in Thailand's business world. Most of Japan's foreign trade is handled by the *shoji*. Recently, the *shoji* have made great inroads into Thailand's foreign trade business. If this trend is not checked immediately, the potential of local entrepreneurs in the field of foreign trade will be greatly inhibited.

Another question analysed in this study is the degree of control the governments of Japan and Thailand exercise over their national economies. It shows that the governments of both countries directly or indirectly influence their economies in different ways. In Japan, the government is dependent on big business, whereas in Thailand, military leaders and high ranking bureaucrats are recruited by big business to protect its interests. Thus, interdependent relationships between big business and the government exist in both countries.

Having made such comparisons which are essential to a better understanding of patterns of economic interaction between the two countries, the study goes on to consider economic relations between Japan and Thailand and Japanese economic activities in Thailand.

Trade Relations. Thai-Japanese trade began in the early seventeenth century at the latest. At present (1973), Japan is Thailand's largest trading partner. As Thailand's foreign trade increasingly depends on Japan, Japan's trading dependency on Thailand is declining. Trade imbalance in favor of Japan began in 1954. Since then, Thailand's trade deficit with Japan has increased from year to year (6,387 million baht in 1973). This has constituted one of the major factors leading to anti-Japanese feeling among the Thai people. Attempts have been made at the governmental level to correct the situation, but an effective solution has yet to be devised.

Economic Cooperation. Although the benefits and the amount of net gain from overall economic cooperation between Thailand and Japan are difficult to assess, Japan's account book clearly shows a credit in its economic cooperation with Thailand. Economic cooperation takes several forms, but the more dominant ones are Japanese assistance to Thailand in the form of loans and technical assistance. Loans were negotiated on two occasions, one in 1968 and the other 1972. The first loan amounted to 1,200 million baht and the second one, 4,500 million baht. The annual interest ranged from 4.5% to 5.75% for the first loan, and for the second, from 3.25% to 5.25%. Both loans were originally given with strings attached, i.e. requiring imported goods and services to come from Japan. However, the strings of the second loan were removed following unfavorable reactions from Thai youth. (It was announced also in

December 1973 that the annual interest rate of a certain unimplemented loan project was to be reduced to 2.75%).

Japanese technical assistance to Thailand has increased significantly in recent years. This category of assistance included financing personnel of government and related agencies as well as students and Thai business employees for training in Japan; Japanese experts sent to assist Thailand in various development projects were also included. Thailand has ranked third among Asian countries (next to Indonesia and the Philippines) as a recipient of Japanese technical aid which mostly belong to the so-called "official development assistance."

Economic Machine. Japanese economic activities in Thailand are generally approved by the Japanese government. The government agencies closely involved in the matter are the Ministries of Foreign Affairs, International Trade and Industry, and Finance. Economic relations feature dominantly in the activities of the Japanese Embassy in Bangkok. Propaganda and cultural activities are handled through the Japanese Information Service. Other agencies, official and unofficial, set up in Bangkok to promote mutual interests or Japanese interests include the JETRO, the Japanese Chamber of Commerce, the Overseas Technical Cooperation Agency, the Overseas Economic Cooperation Fund, the Export-Import Bank of Japan, etc. They help smooth and accelerate Japanese-Thai economic interactions and expand Japanese economic activities in Thailand.

Japanese Investment. Thailand's social, political, and economic climate is conducive to Japanese investment. At present (1973) Japanese investment ranks first among foreign investments in terms of the amount of capital and the number of enterprises. In the industrial sector, Japanese investment is heavily concentrated on the labor intensive textile industry.

Most Japanese investments are in the forms of joint ventures. Japanese shares in the joint venture, in terms of capital and management, are arranged to suit the partner's expertise and interests. Because they possess higher managerial, technical, and marketing skills, the Japanese partners tend to hold key positions in most joint ventures, leaving some ceremonial posts and personnel direction to the local Thais.

The transfer of managerial and technical skills has been gradual and natural. The demands for speeding such a transfer are essentially coming from outsiders rather than the Thai partners. The Japanese partners are prepared gradually to transfer part of their responsibilities to the Thai partners, as they determinedly diversify their investment activities by creating new enterprises.

The expansion of Japanese investment has constituted one of the main factors that has caused the Thais to fear Japanese economic domination and the importation of industrial pollution.

As other business enterprises in Thailand, the Japanese/Japanese-Thai ventures attempt to maximize their profits even at the expense of legality. Malpractices are not without the surreptitious cooperation of Thai partners and unscrupulous Thai authorities.

The partners and top executives in the joint venture are generally satisfied with the situation. They claim that the Japanese investors deserve what they gain, and the arrangements in the enterprises are justified. Such arguments are not subscribed to by most skilled and semi-skilled Thai employees who quietly protest against the unfair share of profit and management they and their Thai compatriots are given. The unskilled laborers, on the other hand, do not normally think about these problems.

By the end of 1972, there were about 6,000 to 8,000 Japanese in Thailand. Many of them entered Thailand as tourists. They usually renew their visas to stay in Thailand by going to neighboring countries and re-entering or by sending "gifts" to immigration officers.

Most Japanese in Thailand are highly educated. About 90% of them speak English but only 30% speak Thai. Those who speak Thai usually work at the production level. The Japanese come to work in Thailand by rotation. The senior ones tend to regard the assignment as an overseas trip reward. The young and ambitious ones do not usually enjoy the stay, however. Those who have responsibilities for their children's education want to return to Japan as soon as they enter Thailand.

Japanese personnel are paid as in Japan. Some receive extra allowances. These practices help preserve Japanese apartness and are not as congenial to integration as the practices of other Asian nationals living in Thailand.

A survey of the business activities of eight giant Japanese general trading companies (shoji) indicates that these companies have gradually and naturally built up their firms in Thailand as economic satellites. By virtue of their better organizational skills, better marketing networks, and stronger capital, the powerful companies threaten Thailand's existing economic system. They tend to monopolize Thailand's internal and external trade. If no proper measures are taken to prevent the trend of their expansion, in the long run, the local people will be unable to develop their potential in business, especially in international trade.

The Japanese are also active in the fields of **banking and financial institutions.** At present (1973), there are two Japanese banks (Tokyo and Mitsui) and six Japanese-Thai financial institutions. Most Japanese/Japanese-Thai business firms open their accounts at either one or both of the Japanese banks. The banks enjoy equal rights with other local banks, which is quite unusual for a foreign bank. Financial institutions are operating as freely as trading firms. Because there is no securities market in Thailand, financial institutions are viewed in economic terms as healthy for Thailand's economy, for they help to mobilize capital for industrial development, but as this field is still neglected by Thais, it is recommended that the government beware the consequences of their financial power and ability to control and regulate marketing and prices.

Many of the undesirable Japanese activities relate to the **service sector:** shipping, advertising, tourist business, restaurants, and entertainment. The shipping business contributes very little to Thailand's economy: it practises tax evasion and bribery, and adopts the attitude of non-integration to Thai society. The advertising business contributes a great deal to Thailand's trade deficit. It helps promote consumer values suited to the Japanese life style among the Thai people. The government receives no tax from this business because all advertising companies operate at a loss. Tourist agencies are one of the most profitable businesses in Thailand. Some ten agencies are owned or partly shared by the Japanese. They hire over 2,000 Japanese as tourist guides and this, illegally, as foreigners are prohibited by law from working as tourist guides. Bribery and tax evasion are part of their business practices. In many respects, they do not help the Japanese tourists to understand Thailand as it is, but are inclined to introduce the dark side of Thailand's night life to the visitors. The main objective is no other than making money. There are many restaurants and entertainment businesses invested in by the Japanese. They pay few legal fees to the government but much tea money to local officials. In some places, the Japanese customers can use checks issued in Japan. One wonders if Thailand is not a Japanese colony. Does Bangkok still need Japanese investment in the semi-brothel business of Turkish baths and cabarets?

Problems and Solutions. As economic interaction is getting more extensive, incidents of conflict are also increasing. The past two years (1972-1973) brought out many aspects of conflict in the pattern of the Japanese-Thai relationship. Many Thai critics, with the university students and mass media at the forefront, are not happy with the existing patterns of economic interaction. This was demonstrated against from November 20 to 30, 1972, by the much publicized mass campaign called "The Anti-Japanese Goods Week Campaign," sponsored by the National Students' Center of Thailand.

The sources of conflicts are numerous, but one basic element lies in the selfishness of individuals (some Thai and some Japanese) who callously and unscrupulously strive to maximize their gains, thinking of their self interest more than the common interest. Their drive for self interest is countered by the emerging forces of the idealistic and enlightened youth of Thailand. The existing political mechanisms are incapable of resolving the conflicts and it is expected that incidents of conflict will be endemic. The conflicts can be minimized, however, if both Thais and Japanese attempt to resolve problems in good faith. For the Thais, they should improve their trade imbalance with Japan by abandoning their habit of luxury, diversifying export markets, bargaining with the Japanese businessmen in an organized effort, imposing import control measures on certain commodities, recruiting commercially-minded businessmen into government foreign trade organizations, and strictly controlling foreign-trade business. As for the Japanese investment in Thailand, the Thais should take initiative in improving any undesirable effect by strictly controlling all foreign investments; laying down measures to facilitate transfer of technical and managerial skill, to investigate bribery, to control profiteering, economic empire building, and advertising; prohibiting foreign investment in the service sector and foreign banks from receiving money deposit. The Japanese, on the other hand, should be sympathetic with the financially and organizationally weaker Thais, and should be mutually responsible for their own practices as stipulated in the Japanese initiated ethical code of conduct. On the question of Japanese-Thai trade, the Japanese businessmen should give more consideration to human factors, less to material gains, be more modest in advertising activity, avoid cut-throat competition with the Thai entrepreneurs, restrict certain export commodities to Thailand, and buy more Thai agricultural products. As for the investments, the Japanese/Japanese-Thai firms in Thailand should readjust their relation with their headquarters in Japan so as to give the former greater autonomy. The Japanese/Japanese-Thai ventures should refrain from increasingly making the Thai economy dependent on the Japanese economy. Above all, both Thais and Japanese should be optimistic, trustworthy, and sincere in their business dealings. One should not take it for granted that economic gains Thailand receives from Japan by any means would be automatically reciprocated by friendship. More essential to friendly relations are the reduction of the Japanese presence and influence in Thailand. In the final analysis, the cost of friendship is no less than the gradual "Thailandization" of Japanese economic presence in Thailand.

Chapter 22: Problems and Proposals

1. *General:* The majority of the Thai people are presently dissatisfied with the existing Japanese-Thai economic interaction. This discontentment is evident among the politically-minded Thais. Under the current economic interaction, the Thai people realize that they are greatly dependent on the Japanese. Initially, this dependence was voluntary but, now, it has become involuntary. The Japanese-Thai interaction should not be allowed to remain in the present state, however, one must admit that, through either temperament or reason, it has remained this way. The situation can be

rectified only through corrective measures as well as by establishing a better understanding. The following are proposals and recommendations, which the Thai side and the Japanese side should follow:

2. *Proposals for the Thai side*

   2.1 *Trade*

   2.1.1 *Curtailment of extravagance:* One of the causes of Thailand's heavy loss in its balance of trade is its lower production power, while its consumption power is much in excess of the level of its economic progress. The major reason for this is partly that numerous Thai people are ostentatious and extravagant, along with the fact that the foreign military men as well as the aliens in Thailand (excluding the Asian people with the exception of the Japanese) are fond of consuming foreign goods, thus causing Thailand to purchase more goods from foreign countries. In this connection, an anti-extravagance campaign should be launched, and seizure of the commodity markets in all foreign military quarters and communities should be made in order to force them to buy Thai goods, especially those which Thailand can produce.

   2.1.2 *Expansion of the trade market:* Thai tradesmen (both importers and exporters) are having to rely increasingly on business transactions with the Japanese because the Thai market is limited. In this instance, Thailand should expand its trade markets, such as open trade with the People's Republic of China and other nations and pay less attention to the differences in political ideologies.

   2.1.3 *Association:* Thai merchants should establish a stronger coalition. The government should promote and not prohibit the coalition of merchants. The uniting of merchants in domestic trade may bring about positive as well as negative results. It may be bad if the merchants band together to set the price of commodities, but there may be good results if the government diplomatically deals with the groups of merchants and allows them to set controls on prices of commodities. In the case of the association of merchants engaged in foreign trade, the good effects on the nation will have greater impact than the bad. The associated merchants may use their joint bargaining power against the Japanese group so there would be no competition among themselves in the purchase as well as in the sale of goods to and from foreign nations. In the past, this competition in sales helped the Japanese to hold down the price of Thai products, while competition in purchasing resulted in our buying goods at prices higher than normal.

   2.1.4 *Application of measures for control of certain imported commodities:* Thailand should prohibit the import of certain luxury goods, or fix quotas for the import of luxury goods from each country. Classification of goods to come under the luxury category should be made yearly under the free economic system. It is desirable that the import and export restrictions be freely done. The abstention from buying foreign goods should be a matter of inducement rather than that of force. No one dares to say that the economic system of Japan is not a free one, but nevertheless there is the fixture of quotas for imports in Japan. This means that the export is free but import is not. Nevertheless, Thailand has no right, according to international practice or by moral standard, to tell the Japanese government to revoke its import quotas as that would be an offence against its sovereignty. Thailand has the right to react in the same manner; we can prohibit the import of foreign goods.

Certain luxury goods, such as shark's fin, ginseng, cosmetics, carpets, antiques, sporting goods, sound recorders, record players, including various luxury automobiles, should be brought under import restrictions. Many Thai people, especially the rich, are competing with each other in the display of their wealth, regardless of the possible downfall of the country.

2.1.5 *Use of commercial-minded men in place of government officials:* The Thai government and the merchants should more actively cooperate in finding markets and procuring data for international trade. Thai officials in general are not suitable for the trading business. They may be good at doing commercial research work. Being a good merchant has nothing to do with possessing any academic degrees. Therefore, the Ministry of Commerce should introduce a new system in its working mechanism by bringing in efficient traders from the business circles to work cooperatively. Thai assistant economic or commercial attachés in foreign countries should have a trading background.

2.1.6 *Strive hard:* The Thai government will have to work harder in its trade negotiations with the Japanese government. It is well known that the Japanese possess a lot of finesse and experience in trade negotiations. In addition they have in hand various pertinent data, whereas the Thais lack sufficient data and the time to prepare themselves well for trade negotiations, and are engulfed in red tape.

2.1.7 *Application of measures for control of import-export companies:* The import-export business is the type of business which should be controlled by the government. Foreign companies (having foreign shares in excess of 50 percent) should not be allowed to engage in this type of business and foreign traders should be required to register with the Ministry of Commerce specifying their business. Formerly, goods from Japan were almost entirely imported by the Japanese or Thai-Japanese companies. Sometimes, goods were imported not because of their demand, but because they had been brought in, advertising campaigns were launched to create a demand.

2.2 *Investment*

2.2.1 *The Thai government should begin revision of investment policy:* The Thai side should admit that it has been through its initial free trade policy that the present huge Japanese investment in Thailand has resulted. The granting of special promotional privileges in connection with the promoted Japanese investments has come from the Thai side. Such being the case, when undesirable results appear, it should be the Thai side that implements the corrective measures. The government should consider the revision of its investment policy an important task.

2.2.2. *Government control:* Foreign investment is a good thing but the Thais should not be so greedy as to permit establishments which cause environmental pollution. Japanese investments in Thailand have contributed to Thai economic development, assisted in increasing labour employment, and helped the Thai people to gain more knowledge. But, the government should have close control of those enterprises, where foreigners have joint ownership, in order to prevent foreigners from outdoing Thai products in the form of competition, and to prevent foreign companies from monopolizing or engaging in business which tends to destroy the business potential of the Thais.

2.2.3 *To lay down measures for imparting technology and management concepts:* The government should lay down measures for the control of foreign enterprises, including those wholly or partly owned by the Japanese, so as to induce them to impart to the Thais technological know-how and management concepts more quickly than is being done at present.

2.2.4 *To lay down measures for control of profiteering:* The government should control the financial activities of foreign companies, including the Japanese companies and those jointly owned by the Japanese, by regularly inspecting their income and payment accounts as well as their profits. The government should also find a way of dealing with companies engaged in profiteering.

2.2.5 *Protection against establishment of economic imperialism:* The government should formulate protective measures against the establishment of economic imperialism, which makes the Thais satellites of the Japanese companies in Thailand, so that they will in turn become satellites of the parent-company in Japan. This is a monopoly system which the Thais do not want.

2.2.6 *To investigate bribery:* The Thai people should be on the lookout for Thai officials who misappropriate monies or accept bribes from Japanese or Thai-Japanese enterprises. Through a survey, it was discovered that a number of Thai officials have been underhandedly earning money from Japanese companies. Those people have sold Thai benefits to the Japanese, thus triggering a feud between the Thai and the Japanese people, who are not concerned with such benefits.

2.2.7 *Prohibition of investment in service business:* The Thai government should restrict investment by aliens in service business activities. The activities of the Japanese banks and financial institutions should be restricted (not prohibited). In the insurance and transportation businesses, foreigners should not hold more than an individual 10 percent of the total share capital, and not more than 50 percent collectively. A protection must be made against the subsequent gradual purchases of shares by foreigners. In addition, control of the business should be in the hands of the Thais.

2.2.8 *Control of advertisements:* If it is impractical to control below 50 percent of foreign shares, then investments by aliens in these businesses should be altogether prohibited, as it would be of no advantage to our economic system. Furthermore, the Thai partners should actually handle the advertising jobs in the joint-venture companies, and the Japanese should not be allowed to use their Thai partners' names only to set up the companies. Also, the mass media, particularly TV stations, should be prohibited from transacting with wholly Japanese and Thai-Japanese companies for the purchase of cheap TV films, which have a bad influence on Thai children.

2.2.9 *To prohibit foreign investment in the restaurant and night-club business:* Foreigners should be prohibited from investing in the restaurant and night-club business. However, they can be employed as chefs, but on a limited scale.

3. *Proposals for the Japanese side*

   3.1 *General*

   3.1.1 *To think less of legal rights:* It should be the task of the Thais to present to their Japanese counterparts certain matters for the latter's revision and improvement. However, the Japanese should understand the feebleness of the Thai social and economic structure and therefore should help the Thais by making some revisions. Japanese assistance in this regard should manifest their sympathy and moral obligation rather than their lawful duty.

   3.1.2 *To understand the Thai mentality:* The Japanese should understand that the Thais are lacking in knowledge because they know very little about the Japanese people. However, the Thai people know that inequality exists in their relationship with the Japanese. As a result, their actions are only an expression of dissatisfaction. However, the Japanese are asked to understand the mentality of the Thais, who are at a disadvantage.

   3.1.3 *To give and take:* The Thai-Japanese economic interaction is in a form which will bring about advantages to both parties. From the economic point of view, Japan is better off as it is in Thailand than it would be if Thailand were colonized as Japan had colonized other countries during the Second World War, because Japan need not employ a great number of soldiers for its control as in the case of a colony. The colonized natives, rankled by their defeat by the Japanese, usually were uncooperative and did not render economic advantages to Japan. In view of this fact, although the Japanese have more bargaining power, they have to deal with Thailand in a "give and take" manner. The result is that Japan will have its share in making Thailand rich while Japan itself will become richer. In this manner, Thai people will feel less indebted to Japan, in the same manner as Japan felt indebted to the United States. If the Japanese investors had undertaken to establish joint investments with the Thais, without too much control and dictation, Japanese business would have been reasonably welcome.

3.1.4 *Control of conduct among themselves:* The control of Japanese businessmen by the Japan Foreign Trade Council and other organizations is worthy of praise. Japanese businessmen are requested to help each other to clarify obscure points in the practice of trade. On May 10, 1973, the Japanese Foreign Trade Council recommended that major general trading companies consider the advantages and living conditions of the public in their business transactions and be sympathetic and lend assistance to one another. On June 1, 1973, the Japan Federation of Economic Organizations, the Japan Chamber of Commerce and Industry, the Japan Committee for Economic Development, the Japan Federation of Employers' Associations, and the Japan Foreign Trade Council jointly announced their proposals and guidance for the practice of trade in connection with the development of undeveloped countries. The guidance consists of nine points, which briefly are as follows:

(1) Behave oneself so as to gain a favourable welcome and settle down permanently in the host country. Maintain good relations with the host country and be a part of local society.

(2) Promote business on the basis of trust in one another. For instance, give the local people the opportunity to have their share in the business increased within a reasonable period of time.

(3) Increase the number of locals employed and promote local workers, as well as improve working conditions and the sanitation of work units.

(4) Select officers who are suitable for working in overseas enterprises and arrange for training.

(5) Try to impart knowledge and experience to local workers, such as by arranging for training in the work units or by sending workers to Japan for training.

(6) Try to use local products for the purpose of promoting other industries.

(7) Re-invest profits in the host country.

(8) Co-operate with the host country in refraining from the combination of industries.

(9) Establish tranquility with the host country by assisting host country citizens to maintain a clean environment, by promoting education and public welfare, and by establishing joint ventures with the local people.

3.1.5 *Seeing each other's heart:* The Japanese should understand that they have built their nation without concerning themselves with other nations and what other nations think about Japan. This indicates the superiority of the Japanese, particularly enhanced by the independent development of their internal economy. However, since they have to depend on other nations, they must try to change their attitude in this respect.

3.2 Trade

3.2.1 *Don't look only at the market:* The Japanese should look not only at the market but also at the people. The Thais are sentimental people and expect reciprocation in kind from their trading partners. They have usually received such reciprocation from Chinese merchants. Nonetheless, the Japanese tend to look at Asia and see only the trading markets. In the case of Japan having suddenly recognized the People's Republic of China and abandoning Taiwan, there were several reasons for its action. However, in the opinion of the Thai people, Japan seems to be in need of a bigger market.

3.2.2. *Don't make too many all-out sales campaigns:* Japanese people are no worse than other nationals in their desire to sell their goods in the largest quantities, but the Japanese have made greater attempts than other nationals and have sometimes used more unscrupulous means than others. Japanese merchants are fond of telling their Thai counterparts that Thai products are not in accordance with Japanese tastes. They ask the Thais to try to improve the form, type, quality, etc. of their products. At the same time Japan sends plenty of goods to Thailand without considering whether they are to the taste of the Thai people. The Japanese pay no attention to this point but resort to changing the taste of the Thais through the media of advertisement.

3.2.3 *Competition in establishing markets in Thailand inadvisable:* Economic activity is similar to political activity on one point. Wherever the big powers get into competition, there will usually be havoc there. The gigantic Japanese companies in Thailand should not compete in establishing their affiliates and in purchases and sales in order to obtain competitive business figures. They should limit their activities in order to let local companies have the opportunity of progressing and expanding.

3.2.4 *Let certain goods exportable to Thailand be limited:* This proposal appears to be astonishing since it is the right of Thailand to restrict imports into the country. It was so proposed because this matter requires the cooperation of both sides to make controls effective. Japan has yielded to twelve countries in Western Europe in their prohibition of its export of tape-recorders to compete in the European market since November 2, 1972. This shows that even the countries which have effective political systems dare not undertake the prohibition of the import of Japanese goods on their own without the cooperation of the Japanese government. The same consideration should be made on certain luxury commodities exported by Japan to Thailand, but the matter should be initiated by the Thais, by submitting a list of luxury goods required for import restrictions to the three-level meetings which take place annually. In this connection, the Thai Ministry of Commerce must research the demand of the market in Thailand for the quantity of each individual item of such goods to be purchased from any country.

3.2.5 *More agricultural products be purchased from Thailand:* Tapioca products, pineapples and other fruits should be purchased more by Japan. A great many agricultural products are restricted for import into Japan for the protection of domestic producers. This is the justifiable right of the Japanese nation, which Thailand cannot interfere with, but under the available import quotas, Japan is requested to buy as many goods as possible from the countries which are losing the most in their trade balance with Japan, such as Thailand.

3.2.6 *Japanese should not engage in destructive competition against Thais:* Thai traders who trade with foreign countries are already limited in number, because large Japanese companies have snatched the businesses from them due to bigger capitals and better business networks. Japanese merchants are in the position to make Thai traders go bankrupt. The price undercutting tactic of the Japanese for the purpose of monopolizing purchase/sale transactions was practised on Thailand in the case of the sales of fluorite ore to Soviet Russia. Japan should not launch such unscrupulous trade practices against Thailand. The Thai people may someday be so infuriated by such unscrupulous acts that they may exercise their right to drive the Japanese out of their country.

3.3 *Investment*

3.3.1 *To improve relations between mother companies in Japan and their branches in Thailand:* The former president of the Japan Chamber of Commerce once stated: "A Japanese businessman overseas is like a puppet." Such a concept of the relationship between the overseas Japanese businessman and the host nation should be altered. Representatives of Japanese firms should stay in Thailand for longer periods of time in order that they may better understand the mentality of the Thai people. The mother companies should listen to the opinions of their representatives in Thailand more closely for the improvement of their business in this country.

3.3.2 *Don't expand business by monopolizing:* The Japanese are a homogeneous race, a type of people who are prone to combine and amalgamate their business activities. This quality is rarely found in other nationals but to the Japanese it comes naturally. The various companies which combine into groups become affiliates and followers. In some countries, such monopolization is regulated by the law, but these regulations have proven to be not very effective. It is alarming that there is no law against monopolization in Thailand. In the absence of such a law the Japanese should not make it a point to exert every effort towards monopolization. There is a Japanese-owned sugar mill, which has expanded its business to a sugar plantation, purchased land, and is now selling sugar as well. It wants to control all phases of the business. It is quite natural that large companies with a lot of capital can and do wish to expand their businesses, but such an economic expansion does great injustice to local businessmen, who must be protected.

3.3.3 *Don't expand business for Thailand to become dependent on Japan:* In fact, investment in Thailand will contribute to the industrialization of Thailand, but, at the same time, the expansion of industry which must depend on capital goods from Japan in great proportion, will render the Thai economic system increasingly dependent on Japan.

From the Japanese point of view, interdependence in the economic field is desirable and is the objective of the economic policy of Japan. This has made the Japanese seldom realize their mistake in liberally investing in Thailand to such an extent as to make the Thai economy dependent on Japan. Such an action, in the opinion of the Thai public, is considered a plot by the Japanese to take control of the Thai economy through their investments in Thailand.

4. *Proposals for Thais and Japanese*

4.1 *To know each other better:* If there were no connections between us, there would be no harm in not knowing about each other. But the Thais and the Japanese have a lot of connections and both parties understand each other very little. The educational systems of the two countries cannot keep pace with the speedy rate of the increase of connections. The ancestries of the people of these two nations have differences which must be studied and understood each by the other.

The Japanese people, in general, are fond of behaving ostentatiously in the developed countries, exhibiting the attitude that the Japanese do not need the Thais as much as the Thais need the Japanese. No matter whether or not this statement is true, the Thai people are prone to think that the Japanese are proud. The Japanese have the problem of behaving themselves. The survey by Sophia University in June, 1972, revealed that the Japanese feel that they are closer to the United States and Western Europe in a social and cultural sphere than to countries in Asia (this was the result of 50.2 percent of all replies; the replies of the opposite opinion represented 22.2 percent of the whole).

The Japanese are especially regarded by the Thai people, quite differently from the way the European and American people are viewed. The Thai people in general (with some exceptions) look at the Japanese as Asians and expect them to have the same behaviour as the Thais or the Chinese. Therefore, when the Japanese people have not acted in accordance with what is expected, they are not forgiven. As for the Europeans, the Thais have admitted that they are superior to themselves. Although the Thais admit that Japan has made great economic progress, they have never agreed that the Japanese are superior to them in general. Such an opinion follows perhaps from the fact that the Thai people have always thought they are superior to neighbouring peoples such as Cambodia, Laos, etc., and Thailand has never been a colony of any country. Hence, they do not recognize the Japanese as superior, or at least they regard themselves as being equal to the Japanese, and on the whole, a certain amount of friction between the two peoples still exists.

This is a matter of social psychology, whereby both parties may have to re-examine themselves as to what they are — to know themselves fully, and to understand their fellow human beings living in the same world. On the part of the economic leaders, they have a duty to their people to create the best possible atmosphere of harmony and accord.

4.2 *To have more trust in each other:* The Thais are inclined to be suspicious of the Japanese, and the Japanese also do not trust the Thais. Both have their reasons. The Japanese descend from a serious, warrior-like and diligent working class of people. They have been trained to be wise and sagacious. When they want to take advantage of others, they can do so with the use of their capabilities. But the Thai people are somewhat easy-going. When they wish to take advantage of others, they will do so in a more straightforward way. This can be seen from an observation of the attitudes of Thai and Japanese staff in joint-venture companies. The majority of the members of the Thai staff think that they should be in better positions than they are now, while the Japanese staff admits that the Thais have the ability to carry out their current work, but there is a problem of their trustworthiness.

In this connection, the Thais have to prove that they are trustworthy and responsible, and, accordingly, the Japanese have also to employ Thais who have proven their reliability, to work with those in important positions.

4.3 *To look at the future from an optimistic point of view:* The Thais should not be anxious initially to misjudge the Japanese. The Japanese seen by the Thais may not be the real "image" of the Japanese as a whole. The Japanese realize that they themselves were poor people for a long time and are anxious to raise themselves quickly from poverty; this results in a lack of delicacy in building up good relationships with others. In view of this fact, should the Japanese achieve their aim of "instant" prosperity, they may be much more tolerant and agreeable towards their neighbours. The Thais should consider the changes in the Japanese people over the past two years, and it may be hoped that in the future, Thais will live side by side with the Japanese as mutual friends.

4.4 *Too many Japanese should not be allowed to stay in Thailand:* Through either reason or temperament, the Thai people are suspicious of the Japanese. Hence, the immigration of more Japanese into Thailand may further increase the problem. Besides, the Thai people do not seem to be able to see that the trouble caused by the Japanese is not caused by each individual but is the result of the Japanese collectively. Japan has a policy of free departure of its people from the country. The responsibility for restricting the number of immigrants lies with Thailand. In this matter, amicable arrangements should be as follows: On the Japanese side, control should be made of the behaviour of the Japanese people who may discredit Thailand. On the Thai side, strict control is to be made over the number of non-immigrants holding tourist passports — those who have to leave the country monthly to renew their tourist visas, or those who offer bribes to Thai authorities for passport visa renewals. Those coming in to work temporarily tend not to act in a responsible manner as well as those who are here semi-permanently. On the part of either the Japanese or the Thais, if and when anyone is found to be doing things which may be detrimental to the relations between Thailand and Japan, he should be held for prompt return to the country concerned.

4.5 *Let income-earners pay taxes without exceptions:* According to the Thailand-Japan Revenue Agreement, clause 10, a person of the nationality of the country of the contracted party, coming to work temporarily in other contracted party's country, is not liable to payment of income taxes. We understand that not many Thai people in Japan have received tax-payment privileges, but it was found out that plenty of Japanese nationals, who came to work here as non-immigrants, holding tourist passports, do not pay income taxes. The Thai government should find a way to cancel this agreement.

4.6 *Thailand not to adopt the Japanese mode of economic development:* Japan is proud of its experience in economic development and thinks that the Thai people ought to be satisfied with Japanese investment in Thailand which is developing the Thai economy. However, the results have not been as expected because the Japanese form of economic development over a certain period of time will bring about a great disparity in the distribution of wealth. In Thailand at present, the call for equality is a kind of ideal which has great influence. There are many social leaders who are resisting progress by measuring it by material on G.N.P. Presently, a great many people want factories but do not want refuse. They do not want to see development from the economic point of view. Hence, in all investments, both Thai and Japanese capitalists must be aware of the adverse effects which may be brought on society. If Japanese capitalists invest in such a way as to create environmental pollution, those who do not stand to gain directly from the investment may use the results of the investment to remove the Japanese from the country.

4.7 *Japanese goods to be "changed" into Thai goods:* The Thai government should lay down measures for gradual assimilation of the Japanese companies (Thailandization) — not to let Japanese capital and Japanese nationals absorb the business activities of the Thai people (Japanization). Technological knowledge should be imparted and management techniques should be transferred to Thai nationals. Apart from the branches of Japanese companies which are conducting business on a limited scale, officers for permanent attendance should be appointed, and exchange of officers should be discontinued. Obviously, all profits made by Japanese firms are sent back to the mother country. The Thais have always reacted unfavourably towards the Chinese sending money back to China. Now, there is no problem in this regard because the remittance of money back to the Chinese mainland has been greatly reduced. If the Japanese live in Thailand for a long time, they will mix and blend with Thai society as the Chinese nationals in Thailand did. There will be no reaction and resistance. As it is, Japanese nationals in various companies have had no inclination to mix and blend with Thai society and have only been waiting to return to their motherland. This has made them see no necessity in keeping in regular private contact with the Thais.

4.8 *Japan to give only interest-free loans to Thailand:* The majority of the Thai people do not admit that a loan of money with interest is an assistance. So, the more loans given to Thailand, the greater the loss of Japan's popularity and admiration among the Thai people. There is a feeling among the Thais in general that Japan is in the habit of offering loans to Thailand for the purchase of Japanese goods, when Thailand is in an unsound economic situation. It is true that Japanese businessmen have received various loans to buy goods from their own people, and the Thai government will benefit. However, the Thai public does not believe that Japan has good intentions for Thailand, for all they know is that they themselves and their children have to bear the burden of debts with overwhelming interest. Normally, they are justified, because government performance of this nature has never been sanctioned by them. Their government's administrative structure is different from Japan's.

4.9 *To assist in controlling monetary power:* Small companies with the tendency not to be responsible for large companies, often expand the market and their businesses. Profit-making is the way of traders, but they should realize that consideration of their common interest will bring about long-lasting advantages, and this will contribute to the development of friendship between the two countries. It is obligatory to help each other to be aware of and be able to suppress bribery by businessmen.